THE
LAST PADILLA STANDING

My Biography, My Past, My Son

By
Joseph Padilla

© COPYRIGHT 2025 BY JOSEPH PADILLA

ISBN: 978-1-959449-50-8

All rights reserved. No part of this book may be reproduced or transmitted in any form or by any means, electronic or mechanical, including photocopying, recording, or by any information storage and retrieval system, without permission in writing from the copyright owner.

The views expressed in this work are solely those of the author and do not necessarily reflect the views of the publisher, and the publisher disclaims any responsibility for them.

To order additional copies of this book, contact:

Simply Best Reads LLC
39-67 58th Street, 1st floor
Woodside, NY 11377, USA
Phone: (+1 888-203-7688)
simplybestreads.com

Table of Contents

Chapter 1
Tell Me Dad, Who Were You?..2

Chapter 2
Back to Madrid 9

Chapter 3
Madrid to Albuquerque 15

Chapter 4
Holidays in Madrid 20

Chapter 5
Memories of a Cowboy 26

Chapter 6
Somewhere in Time 34

Chapter 7
Madrid, December 7, California 41

Chapter 8
Settling in California From 606 to 5400 - 2B......................48

Chapter 9
Painful Moments...59

Chapter 10
Her Name Was Alta..69

Chapter 11
A Time to Elope 77

Chapter 12
That Little House on the Prairie..81

Chapter 13
TDY—Permanent Temporary Duty 89

Chapter 14

My Last Day of Duty 96
Chapter 15
   A Time to Adjust 100
Chapter 16
   Stolen and Sorrow 106
Chapter 17
   Bureau of Indian Affairs 110
Chapter 18
   B.A.R.T, the Burial, the Money 116
Chapter 19
   Final Chapter: Life Goes On 122

The Last Padilla Standing
My Biography, My Past, My Son

My name is Joseph N. Padilla, better known as Joe by my friends; I was born in 1932 in a coal mining town called Madrid in central New Mexico between Santa Fe, And Albuquerque. The reason I am writing this manuscript is for my son Timothy who wanted to know about our family's past, so he asked me if I would write a biography about my life and the family's history. Sorry to say that he will never see my manuscript, for he passed away on January 30, 2019. He would have been the last male in our Padilla family tree, for I know of no other male persons left in our family to carry on with the family name, and now I am The Last Padilla Standing at the age of 89. I have two daughters left. The family name will be deep in their memories and in time be forgotten. God has his reasons for all life, and I expect that. Now! I will carry on with my son's wish, and on with my biography in memory of my son Timothy Andrew Padilla. Rest in peace, my son.

Chapter 1
Tell Me Dad, Who Were You?

Going back as far as I can remember. My father was named Gabriel; though back then everyone called him Gabe, since my grandfather was also named Gabriel. My father went by Gabriel N. Padilla, using my grandmother's maiden name of Newman as his middle Initial, for he did not have a middle name. Father was a very well-educated man. I was told by him and my grandmother about his schooling back when he was growing up; he graduated from the eighth grade which was as high as the school required back then. He did not go to a regular school; he went to a parochial school in Las Vegas New Mexico, where he graduated from. He continued with his schooling and studied the Latin language. He became an altar-boy there at the Catholic Church in Las Vegas. From learning Latin, he learned a few other languages taken from the Latin method of communication by speech. He spoke English, Spanish, Italian, French, Greek, and other languages taken from his Latin learning; later, he learned to speak Cantonese Chinese; all this I know because I witnessed him speaking with many different people in their own language; all taken from his Latin learning, except for Chinese that I will talk about later. My first memory as a child is how poor we were, I remember the hard times we endured during the great depression. Amazing how I can remember my childhood, but I cannot remember what happened yesterday. Oh, well on with my story. My mother was a very dear and loving person, she was about five foot four inches in height and somewhat plump, a very pleasant and caring mother, who cared so much for my sister and me. Her named was Juanita Segura. (Segura, is the Sir: name of my mother's father.) She was born in the Pueblo De-Sile in New Mexico in the late 1800s; maybe 1899. My mother's family were Spaniards; her family arrived in the United States in the early 1800s. I was told her family landed somewhere in the Caribbean Islands, and on to Florida; and from there too what was known as, The New Spain territory, an organized unincorporated territory with varying boundaries not yet developed until 1821.

As time passed, the family was granted a royal grant by the U S government; the land had been legally established and confirmed by law as required; it was titled under the New Mexico territory bylaws. Sometime later the territory advanced and in 1912 became the state of New Mexico. I believe my history is somewhat correct, as I was told. As for my father's mother, her family hailed from England, around the same time in the early 1800s, her name was Mary Refugio Newman, a very loving person. She became a teacher in a parochial high school in Detroit Michigan, and later in Las Vegas New Mexico; this is where she met and married my grandfather Gabriel Padilla. Her mother, my great-grandmother was named Chanette Newman. I was fortunate to have met my great-grandmother Chanette at the age of 99, I was just a little guy. My father's father was Spaniard, I do not remember much about him, other than that he was a big man. His name was Gabriel Joseph Padilla, and had a brother named Miguel Padilla, my uncle on the Padilla side. He had two daughters, one named, Antonia and his other daughter named Rufina; they were my first cousins on my grandfather Padilla's side of the family. They lived in a very small community called Waldo in New Mexico (now a ghost town); this was the area where The Atchison Topeka, and The Santa Fe took interest in the coal mines of Madrid and made Waldo a central weighing and pick-up station. On the opposite side of Waldo lay a short rail line to Madrid that carried the coal to be transferred to the main line in Los Cerritos. The main road to get to Waldo from Madrid, we had to pass through the small town called Los Cerritos, and from there on to a side road. Some two miles further, we had to climb a huge hill called The Devil Thrown and on down into the valley below where my uncle Miguel lived. The train tracks that ran on the back side of the Madrid hills to Waldo passed by my grandmother's place; the track ran alongside the river's edge that had a walkable trail some eight miles to get to Waldo by foot. This was a private railway to the weighing station from Madrid to Waldo. One memory that comes to mind; one day we went to visit Uncle Miguel, there in Waldo where he lived; they lived on a small hillside just off an old dirt road that went to the coal weighing station where he worked. One day I was told to go get a bucket of water from a natural stream on the hillside; this was the best drinking water that come out of the ground that I had ever drunk; as I was on my way back with the bucket in hand when out of nowhere I was attacked by their dog; he was one huge dog called Jack, black in color with a brown nose, maybe some kind of pit bull and shepherd mix. He came up to me and bit under my left arm and would not let go, all I could do was cry in pain and yelling for mama. They all heard me yelling and came running to where I was, the dog would not release my arm, Uncle Miguel had to slap the dog very hard in order to get him to let go of my arm. I was taken care of, and Uncle Miguel took care of old Jack. Another memory in time. One day we were on the way to visit my uncle Perfecto in a Pueblo called Sile; he was my mother's brother. My mother's family lived in the pueblo just north of Santa Fe called Cochiti. Some two mile or so is the Pueblo called Sile this is where my uncle Perfecto lived. My mother was born there in Sile; they; were the Segura's who have lived there as far back as when the Spaniards were settled in what was known as The New Spain territory, later the territory was changed to The New Mexico territory in the early statehood of the union. My grandfather on my mother's side was named Ciriaco Segura, and my grandmother was named Rafealita Picas before their marriage. My uncle on my mother's side was named Perfecto Segura, his wife, my aunt was named Rafealita; they had three boys and one girl, my cousin Wilford, cousin Raymond, and Cousin Hillel, and my beloved cousin Blanch. I have a great memory of that time in that settlement known as Sile where my uncle Perfecto and his family lived. They were farmers who lived off the land that was shared with the local American natives (Indians). My uncle became blood brothers with the tribal Indians. My grandfather Ciriaco was the Marshall and district agent for all the local tribes. He was well respected and became a blood brother with the tribe by cutting the palm on their hand with a blade and doing a traditional blood handshake. All this I was told by my uncle Perfecto. As a boy, I frolicked and played in just about every acreage of the farming land; I played in the corn fields and in the huge garden fields with my friends. The corn stocks were so tall, the watermelons, and cantaloupes smelled so sweet, the potatoes, the carrots, the green beans, and the green Chile vines flourished, not to forget the beautiful red tomatoes. This was the way they lived and survived. The land was shared with the local pueblo Indians. (American Natives.) At the East end of the farming fields; is where the great Rio Grande River flows; this was the way the farming fields were watered by a unique homemade arrangement. At this river site, my friend and I spent much time playing and looking for frogs and other little critters.

One day we were on our way to the river, as we were passing through the watermelon field, the air was filled with the sweet aroma of sweetness. We decided to take a watermelon knowing that that was a no, no; but we knew that everyone was working on the opposite side of the fields, we felt sure it was safe. We hid behind the corn field where we split the watermelon on a rock and we ate that juicy watermelon; oh, how sweet it was; we buried the leftovers in the soft soil and off we went on to the river. I do not remember my friend's name, but I am almost sure it was Ramon, oh well! That was over 80 years passed. Another moment, I remember, Ramon's mother, she was an extremely large woman (fat) and was with child and her time was at hand, we were told to go play. Once again, we went to the river; we did not know anything about what was to happen. When we decided to go home; as we approached, we noticed the many people around the house; my friend's mother had given birth. Much later I found out that she had had sextuplets, yes six babies; I was told, none lived; we as children did not understand, I found out many years later when mother and I were talking about the incident. I told mother what I was told about the sextuplets. She then told me the story of the sorrowful mishap. As a young boy life was good there at my uncle's house in Sile. It was late-summer and harvest time was at hand; the corn was picked and stored in one of the storage sheds attached to the house, this is where the corn was left to mature until it was ready for husking. Husking corn was a fun time for us kids and the young adult. As the corn was being husked, we sang songs and heard stories from the elders. One night we were all husking corn, sometimes called shucking corn that is, removing the corn kernels from the corncob. The elders would tell spook stories, this was a way to scare the teenagers when they went out after hours and away from the house; this also scared the crap out of me. This is one of the spook stories told to us by my uncle Perfecto. He started telling the story by saying, "Sometime back, - hum! (He uttered), - It was about seven thirty that evening, the family were sitting at the table having supper; it had just gotten dark, and the moon was about, - well, - more than half full, when! Welford came in overly excited and frightened saying that a ghost was trying to get in the back window; this got me a little concerned, so I asked him what he was talking about. Welford was shaking with fear so bad that it made me wonder if he really saw someone or something out back, so I decided to go look; I picked up my double 12-gauge shotgun and I slowly walked around the house to see what he was talking about. It was somewhat darker at the back of the house as I continued; the gang were right behind me. Very quietly, I looked up and saw the ghost about thirty feet away; I then yelled for him to halt, but he wouldn't stop; the ghost kept waving his arms so vibrantly, me knowing what it was, I pretended that I was somewhat scared and I pulled the trigger on my shotgun; I knew who the ghost was; everyone was standing behind me wondering if I had shot the ghost; I then walked forward slowly to see what I had shot, as I stood looking I couldn't hold it any longer and I busted out laughing; the family walked up to me to see why I was laughing so loudly and why this scary thing turn to be a funny moment for me. I slowly walked up to the so-called ghost; you will not believe what I shot? The ghost turned out to be my work shirt and my coveralls full of holes that were waving in the wind that my wife had hung on the clothesline earlier that day. We laughed so hard that tears were running down our cheeks and we had many side aches from the laughter. The family never let my uncle Perfecto live that one down; as for his work clothes! Well, I'll let you figure that one out. This is one of my most joyful memories there. One more adventure comes to mind. Early one morning while on the way to Sile, we were going to visit Uncle Perfecto. A few days back we had a heavy rainfall and the Rio Grande overflooded, and many puddles were left to the sides of the road. On the road just ahead of us, there, in a large puddle Grandpa Ciriaco spotted a large fish flopping in the water, so he told father to stop the horses and go check it out. Grandpa and my father got down off the wagon to look, it was a huge catfish. It was much larger than I was; they placed the fish in the back of the wagon. We started the way the fish was flip and flopping and scaring the horses, grandpa had to hit the fish over the head; and that did stop the fish from flopping. Late that day we had a great feast everyone around were invaded for the fish fry. Oh, happy days.

Chapter 2
Back to Madrid

After a year or so, my father, my mother, and my sister whose name was Mary Francis, and I went back to Madrid. Father was a coal miner and worked in the coal mines ten to twelve hours a day six days a week, with Sunday off. Now, another chapter in my young life. As far as I can remember I was around the age of two maybe three; we lived in a small white house not far from the arroyo facing the upper hill where you could see the schoolhouse in the distance at the upper part of the town. Just across the arroyo is where the railroad tracks were; this is where the Santa Fe locomotive # 769 rested after its daily run; it was called, La-mocha, a Mexican slang word when translated to English meant, Small Engine, or shorty.) The engine would pull some twenty or more coal cars to the transfer station at Waldo some nine or so miles north from Madrid. This small white house is the first house I somewhat remember we lived in. My first memories there are when I was about two, or two and a half years of age, I was playing with the wooden blocks that my grandmother had given to me, I had them placed in line pretending it was the old 769 train across the arroyo, I was so proud that, I had to show mama, by saying, "look mama la pooch-a." Mama turned and asked me what the la pooch-a was? I remember telling her, "You know mama, la pooch-a." she looked at me in wonderment, so I pointed out the window and looking at the engine across the way. I replied: "la fam-fa FAM fa, fam-fa FAM fa, la pooch-a. She looks at me and smiled and she replied, "Oh! La Mo-cha." What a story she had to tell my father when he came in from work. Another time in the same house; we were having supper; back then beans, potatoes, and tortillas were the meal; tortillas were cheap and easy to make back then, white bread, or corn bread would dry and would not last long due to the heat of the day; beans and red Chile was the daily meal, chicken on Sunday maybe once a month due to hard times. I remember sitting in my highchair when my father asked mother to pass him the red Chile; he was putting some Chile in his plate of beans, I wanted some on my beans. Father looked up at mama, I remember the smile on father's face. Mama stood looking up at him and saying, "don't you dare." Papa looked over at me, I was acting up and crying for this red stuff called Chile that he was putting in his plate that he seemed to enjoy very much. My sister Frances was at the end of the table, she knew about Chile, but she did not say anything she just snickered. Papa looked up at mother and said, "Why not?" Mama just looked and shook her head. Papa dipped his spoon into his plate and gave me a taste of his chili beans. I remember how hot it was; you can imagine the disfiguration on my face but, that did not stop me, I wanted more. With tears in my eyes, I ate my beans with Chile, as far back as I can remember I have been eating Chile ever since. As the days passed by, times became awfully hard on my folks, my mother's mother, my grandmother Segura was sick and near death, and father had to take a leave of absence from work. My father had a 1934 Ford coupe with a rumble seat where my sister and I would sit. We moved to Cochiti Pueblo, and we stayed with my mother's family. My grandfather was the Indian agent for all the local Pueblo Indian districts about, and it was hard for him to leave grandma alone in her sick condition, so my parents came to stay with them. I remember Grandma Segura laying extremely sick in her bed. One day, about mid-day my mother and all the local ladies were in the front room waiting for Grandma's hopeful recovery: I was playing on the floor unaware about what was happening. It was a very hot day and the women decided to change grandma's clothing and the sheets on her bed to make her more comfortable. As they were undressing her, I heard her take a big gasp of air then she started shaking violently causing her to urinate, I looked up with an unpleasant state of mind, I saw her urine flow up in the air just before she took her last breath. Though this may sound somewhat strange, for a child, an unusual moment like this will stay in the child's mind. Strange how I remember that moment for it left me with an unusual feeling as to what had just happened that day, for this was my first time that I saw someone pass on. May she rest in peace.

A few days had passed, and the family were having a day of celebration, I, do not remember what Holiday they were celebrating, it could have been a holy day. That day a close neighbor named Tom (Tomas Gomes) from the next house over was to kill a chicken for the dinner that afternoon. The kids and I stood looking and watching Tom as he took the chicken by the neck and started twirling it; around and around went the chicken, when the neck was severed, he stood holding the chicken's neck in hand; as for the poor chicken! It flew up in the air and landed on the top of a tall tree branch, it was funny to see him climbing the tree everyone was laughing. That is all I remember about that trip to Cochiti Pueblo. We went back to Madrid, and father went back to work, and my sister went back to school. When back in town I remember father rented a house at the end of the north side of Madrid near the arroyo where a stream ran through it. The house was nice it had two bedrooms, living room and the kitchen; the house sat on a small hill overlooking the neighborhood and the arroyo, and just across the arroyo is where the railroad tracks lay. One memorable event that happened to me there when I was about six. As you know by now, my father was a coal miner and the miners and only had one day off, it was Sunday, and the only entertainment back then was the radio; father and mother would sit and listen to the nightly news and other pogroms. One evening mom and papa were listening to the Grand Old Opry on the radio, father would have his jug of wine next to the back of his chair and a glass of wine in his hand. I was about five watching him enjoying his wine. Now came wonder boy, yours truly, wondering what this so-called wine that we the children could not have that seems to make father incredibly happy and wondering why we could not have this so-called wine. That evening my sister France and I were playing a game on the floor when a thought came to me! Being so brilliant at an age of wonderment, that brilliant thought hit me! Oh yeah, it was the wine jug behind my father's chair. Father was unaware as to what was about to happen as I crept along the back of his chair and picked up his jug of wine, the jug was somewhat heavy, but with my little hands very carefully I pulled the cork and opened it; I pick it up and I took a swallow, it was somewhat sweet, I believe it was called, Tokay, maybe Port, or Muscatel, it was called something like that. I put the jug back down very quietly and went back to where my sister was, as she sweetly sang to me, "You better not do that, papa going to spank you"; we went back playing. I took another look at the jug, and yep, I creeped back; and once again Father was unaware; I took a couple enormous swallows and went back to where my sister was with a big smile on my face. Just about ten minutes or so, I got extremely sick throwing up; yes, you can say I was drunk. My mother got up very worried as my sister told them what I had done; father busted out laughing. After a good laugh, I was placed in bed and soon I passed out. This must be the reason I do not drink today; a lesson well learned. They never said anything to me about that night, I was never spanked or talked about the incident, and father knew I had learned my Lesson. I am sure my folks must have had a great time telling the story to the family and friends. Another event I remember there in that same neighborhood we moved to a larger old brown house closer to the arroyo. My cousin Lupe at about the age of 17 was living there with us; I was about six or seven. It so happened that a Native American man named, Antonio, hailed from Cochiti Pueblo came by with a load of watermelons and other assorted melons and asked my parents if it was OK to leave the melons and his cart there at our house. He was welcomed. He sold his melons and watermelons throughout Madrid, going from door to door; he left an array of melons, and watermelons at our home using one of the bedrooms. The sweet aroma of the melons filled the house. One day, Cousin Lupe and I were in his room, and he said, "Why don't we take a watermelon Antonio won't know for he has brought so many." I just looked at him with a smile on my face. "Now," he said, "You, take the watermelon to the back window and hand it to me." Knowing that window was a bit high Cousin Lupe convinced me that it was all right to drop the watermelon and that he would catch it; so, done. I quietly sneaked by my mother with a little fear of guilt for she was an ear puller every time I would do something wrong, it is a wonder I can hear today; I walked to the side of the house where my cousin Lupe was waiting for me under the window. He said, "Follow me." We started running towards the train tracks just under the arroyo bridge where we sat on the ground. He cracked the watermelon on a rock; when we finished, he threw the leftovers into the river. We stood there laughing and looking at the leftovers as they flooded downstream. How sweet that watermelon was, and never missed. Many years have passed and I still think about that moment. Another time came to mind; a merchant known to my parents came by; he had a truck with a homemade cover over the truck bed it was somewhat large and very unusual; he was a tinker, a maker of religious idols and wooden crucifixes; he would melt the pot-metal on a large container over a very unusual stove; he would pour the melted liquid in a Jesus mold; when finished he would paint and place the figuring on a cross; a very unusual crafted man. Mama and grandmother fell in love with the crucifixes that the man was making. My father did not have much money to speak of, but! Father had traded with this man many times in the past. The forged bodies of Christ were very carefully crafted, and hand painted then he would place the forged bodies on a black wooden cross, so realistic, he would sell them for two dollars apiece or trade. Not having much money on hand, Father did some horse trading with him; they bickered for a while; father Knowing that the man needed coal for his burner and wisely asked the man about a trade, coal for his ware. The coal was free to all the homes as part of the monthly rentals. A sack of coal for a cross; and grandma traded with him for four blocks of cheese; a done deal. Today I still have the two crucifixes hanging on my wall; I have cherished them for over 80 years hoping my two daughters will honor my memories of their ancestors and take care of these family treasures.

Chapter 3
Madrid to Albuquerque

There is a story on the crucifixes and how one came about later in time. I often wondered what ever happened to the one given to my sister. Up to what I just described, one was given to me by my mother, and the other was given to my sister by my grandmother; all this happened some years after we were old enough to appreciate what they meant. Now going forward in time, it was around the year 2001 when I recovered the one my sister had that I thought was lost. One day while we were visiting my sister, she asked me to go get something from the garage for her; I walked into the garage to get what she wanted, she told me that it was hanging on the wall, when I looked up at the wall, I saw the crucifix that I always wondered whatever had happened to it? Knowing that this cross was given to her by my grandmother many years back. When I went back into the house, I ask her about the crucifix, and why it was hanging in the garage? She told me that she did not believe in a cross with the body of Christ placed on it, telling me that Jesus had risen, and it offended her beliefs. This hurt me some, but I respected her views. After talking with her for a while I asked her if I could have the cross. Without hesitation she said Sure; I believe she knew how much that cross meant to me. I felt like the cross was a lost brother; I love those old crosses in the hopes that the family tradition carries on. Now to go back to my childhood memories. At around late 1938, if my memory has not failed me. It was in this old brown house that I had my first communion. One Sunday after we got home from church, my sister asked father about Jesus? Father took her and I to one of the bedrooms and told us to sit on the edge of the small bed. Just above the bed on the wall was a Baby Jesus statue figurine that was placed on a wooden frame on the wall; father looked at us and started telling us stories of Jesus, and that he is the Son of God; he continued telling the story of the life of Christ. After the story ended; father said, "If you ever need anything, or you need help, just ask Jesus in prayer." Not knowing what prayer was, I just listened. He then looked at us and asked if there was anything we needed or wanted, maybe something - sweet? That is all it took, I looked over at my sister she looked back at me then she said, "Papa, can we ask for candy, - can we papa?" I was all for that. Father knew when he mentioned something sweet that candy would be in mind. Penny candy was seldom affordable back then due to the hard times. Father asked us to get up and kneel in front of the bed and look up at Jesus figure above our head, "now!" he said, "Close your eyes and pray." Me being a child, I did not know what pray meant; so, I asked papa. He then replied, "Son, when you are in need of things you tell Jesus your needs and He will grant your request, but you must be sincere with your asking." That was alright with me I was just waiting for my sister's request to be answered. With our eyes closed, father started saying a prayer, and to this day, I still do not know how papa placed the two pieces of hard rock candy on the feet of Jesus well over our heads without us knowing, for he had to walk a few steps and reach well over our heads to place the candy on the feet of Jesus. I never did ask him, and I still live with that wonderment in mind. Father understood our request for candy, for it was hard times in those depression days; a penny was hard to get back then when other things were more important and necessary. This became my first belief in Jesus and on to this day. With tear-filled eyes, as I write my memoirs that have lingered with me for over 80 years, praise God. It was around that time that my mother was struck sick and had to have her goiter removed. (Swelling in the throat). For her to have the operation, our family had to go to stay with a family relative in Albuquerque where she is to have the operation. We stayed there for a while, maybe three months or so. They were our cousins from my grandmother side of the family on the Newman side. The couple had an unbelievably beautiful daughter named Jo-Ann; she was about 14 years of age. She became my friend and would take me around to meet her friends. One day she was told to go to the store to pick up a few things needed; she invited me to go with her, it was about a block and a half from the house. As we were walking, she was telling me about the things she had to pick up hoping she would not forget anything. When we entered the grocery store, I was so astonished! I had never seen such an array of goodies. As we were walking down the aisle, we approached a table with many eggs on it where one could pick as many eggs as needed. All this brought up another saga in my life as a little boy, remembering how poor we were, and the food shortage was in mind. As I was walking by the table where the eggs were, a thought came about! That is, if I take one of those eggs home it would help with the food shortage in the family! Lucky me no one was looking. Oh yes! With my itty-bitty hand, I picked up an egg and placed it in my itty-bitty blue jacket pocket, I felt sure mama would be proud of me for trying to help with the hunger problems at home. As we walked back, I was so proud knowing that I was helping with the ease of the food shortage in the difficulty of hard times. We arrived home, and I so proudly handed the egg to mother. The first thing mama asked me was, "Where did you get that egg from?" (Ah, - come on I was just a little guy, just wanting to help.) I replied, "I took it from the store when nobody was looking." Uh-Oh! Mother got a hold of my ear and pulling my face right up to hers. As she said. "Young man! You will take that egg right back to the store manager and you will explain to him that you took that egg and your mama made you bring it back because she doesn't want a thief for a son, do you understand?" Still pulling my ear, my ear must have grown at least an inch. Right then my cousin Jo-Ann spoke up and said, "Come I'll go with you." Mama just looked at her and no more was said. Jo-Ann took hold of my hand I could not stop crying with fear that the store manager would spank me and put me in jail. We walked about three houses down when Jo-Ann whispered and said, "Give me that egg." I handed the egg to her, and she said, "Get ready to run." I wondered why she was in such a hurry to run. She took the egg and threw it at the front door of the third house over, then took my hand and said, "Come on, run." We started running. We were about a block away from the house when I asked her why she did that. She looked at me with a big smile on her face and said, "That old witch is always making trouble with us kids around here." I looked at her and said, "What am I going tell Mama?" She replied, "Don't worry I'll tell her that everything went alright." We walked around the block taking our time. I was with fear of what mama would do or say, but I knew Jo-Ann would make up a good story. Well! It was time to face mama in hope she would not pull my ear again. We entered through the back-kitchen door, oh yes, mama was waiting. "Well," she said, "what did the store Clerk say to you?" I started to cry when Jo-Ann spoke up, "The man took the egg and looked down at him and said, 'It takes a lot of will power to admit when you do something wrong and I don't take this very lightly, but you were honest and I will forgive you this time, I think you have learned a good lesson, just don't take anything that doesn't belong to you no matter how much you want it, it may place you in jail.'" Mama just looked down at me and said, "Next time you will have to face your father." Another memory comes to mind while we were there in Albuquerque. It was supper time; everyone was sitting at the table, there was another little girl about the age of four, she was sitting across the table from me; she was an innocent little child named Annie. Sitting quietly, she broke wind; she looked up and said, "Ops; excuses me," then another "Ops; excuse me," and a third; she repeated *excuse me*, every time she passed gas; soon the place was gassed out; as one by one the guests started leaving the table, I also had to leave the table myself, no one said a word. I often wonder if she might still be alive and remembers that event, I hope so. It is so amazing how things from the past can be so defined in the memory of a child of time passed.

Chapter 4
Holidays in Madrid

By now Mother's health was getting better and it was time for us to return to Madrid. When we arrived home, Papa went back to work. Father had a hard time locating a house to rent, so we ended up living in what was called the bonks, an apartment unit unlike normal apartment of today. There were two outhouses across the way that everyone used, and it did not sit very well with my folks, so we used what was called a night potty pot that was used at nighttime, father would dump it out early every morning; the pot was kept in the porch shed for our privacy. We were unable to move due to the house shortage. We lived there for about three months while father waited for a house to rent. With no vacancy to be had the only place my father found was an old double garage just above the baseball park. This was a much better area called Hollywood by many, for it had a view of most of the city of Madrid and the ballpark was just below the homes. This was the area where Uncle Victor lived who told father about the old garage that was empty; father rented the place, and it took a while for them to convert it into a living quarter. I remember my father and Uncle Victor repairing the roof for it leaked like a shower. When they finished converting the garage it was divided into three rooms, a kitchen, a front room, and a bedroom; we lived there for quite a while. After things settled down my father and uncle Victor went on a deer hunting trip, they left about ten in the morning that day; this was strange to me why they left so late in the day. In the past, they would leave at daybreak and returned home a couple of days after nightfall. Early that evening they arrived somewhat early. The deer had been field-stripped and only the meat was brought back for they had field-stripped and cleaned the deer while in the field; another strange thing was, they did not bring the antlers back with them, and as a kid I was, looking forward for the antlers. It was many years after we came to California that my father and I were sitting and talking about old times, when I brought up the deer story back when I was a kid when we lived in what was called Hollywood; he busted out laughing and started telling me the story about the deer; and how hard times were back then and this was a do not ask and do not tell situation, mums were the words back in those days. He giggled lightly with a silly smile on his face, he went on with the story; telling me how hard times were back then and how expensive and scarce beef was, so he and uncle Victor decided to go on that deer hunt; he went on saying that he and uncle Victor drove to an area where a large cattle range that belonged to a local rancher was; it was just a few miles away, and that they had killed one of his calves; no one was around for miles, and when cattle were missing, they would blame the poor local Indians for they had it harder than most. As he went on with the story we sat and laughed; he looked up at me and said, "Best deer meat we ever had." We laughed and giggled for the longest time. Now, back to where we lived in the converted garage; from there my sister walked to school just across the ball Park at the bottom of the small slope. As for me, I was six years of age when I became the caregiver for my mother for my sister was going to school and mother was not to be left alone for a year after her operation some months back, and if anything unusual happened to her I was supposed to go tell our neighbor next door. At that age, those things were unknown to me and that was the reason I started my schooling so late at the age of seven and a half, when I should have been in the second grade not in kindergarten.

The ball park had a tennis court next to it; it was also used as a skating rink. It was there in that old garage we called home when I started my schooling late in my life. The year was 1939, this was my first kindergarten year. That year Ms. Virgilio, my kindergarten teacher had us kids do a Christmas play that was held at the auditorium/theater across the arroyo and just across the road from the old local church. This is so memorable to me for I learned many of the Christmas songs that still hold so dear to me today. After the Christmas celebration, school was back to normal. One day it was play time in the schoolroom, Ms. Virgilio would ask us kids what we wanted to do or play in our free time. I still had the Christmas play in mind so when she asked me what I wanted to do? I told her I wanted to sing; she took it all wrong she though I said swing, and she told me, OK you go swing." I tried very hard to let her know that that was not what I said, and that I wanted to sing, not swing. Her mind was made up, I had to swing, a big misunderstanding between child and teacher. I still remember Miss. Virgilio every Christmas with a smile on my face. Madrid was a very family-orientated town just North of Santa Fe and South of Albuquerque, Madrid was nestled somewhere in the middle. On the west hillside of the town was where the only church there; this is where everybody came to meet for the Sunday morning services, it was a catholic church, but every other religious set went there for it was the only church for miles. Every Easter Sunday after the Sunday service the people would meet in front of the church steps where they gather and start walking to the annual Easter egg hunt that was a about half mile or so from the church; just across the arroyo on the opposite hillside, from there we had to walk up a hill what I believe was called "The Jones mine trail;" this was where the so-called Breaker stood on the hillside, it was where the coal was crushed to size and cleaned before the coal was sold to market. When we reached the top what a surprise! At the top of the trail's end was the most beautiful green acreage never seen by many of us. This was where they had the great Easter hunt annually and looking forward to finding a golden egg that one would receive a silver dollar for it. Unknown to me for many years that it was seven-hole golf course for the upper set, I did not know what golf was, I was maybe eight. Not until we came to California in 1942 while talking with my father; I ask him about the Easter egg hunting field and about the gorgeous green grass? He then told me that this was where the well-to-do would go play Golf and have their picnics. I often wonder where the folks who lived on what was called Front Street and back street did for fun. After the Easter hunt was over, everyone would gather at the playground where the baseball field was. The adults would guide the children in all kinds of events such as, the watermelon eating contest, pie eating contest, and so forth, the winner would receive a silver dollar. I won the watermelon event one year. Uncle Victor on mother's side pressured me to sallow the seeds and eat all the way as close to the watermelon rind as possible, it is one event I will never forget. Winning that silver dollar was like receiving a $20 bill today; we had many different competition events, and sports games back then. Madrid was the first to my knowledge to have night lighting on a baseball field. Madrid had its own power plant, so lighting was no problem there. Many ball teams from many different places or countries came to play ball there. Which comes to mind, I recall, a baseball team from Africa that came to play baseball with the Madrid miners baseball team. They were so comical, one happy bunch, they were a very dark race from somewhere in Africa and truly kind to the children. There were about three or four men in the group with their lips stretched out about four or five inches with a plate under their lips, and they would bounce the ball up and down with their lips. Every child had a great time that day. This is what kids need today, world of entertainment and unity it will live a beautiful memory as the Lord intended us to do so. The ballpark was the town's playground, all celebrations happened there, the parade would start from the south side of town what was called Front Street which led to the playground about half a mile or so; again, as far as I remember, Madrid was a family orientated town. On the main street to the south side at the end of Front Street was what we call a supermarket today, back then we called this, the Company Store. The store sat on an exceptionally large platform above the sidewalk with steps on both sides of the platform. When one entered from the south side it had a large clothing and dry goods section, plus a hardware and home essential needs were. This was the department where Uncle Victor worked. The rear of the store was four feet higher than the main floor this was where the Bank and post office were. Facing to the left was another entrance that went down to the butcher shop and the grocery store; in the center of the grocery store was the main entrance coming from the dry goods section, and right across the center isle was the entrance to the drugstore and an ice cream parlor. This was the soda and ice cream parlor where my grandmother and I spent many times eating a Tommy bar; a Tommy bar was an ice cream bar covered with chocolate. From the drug store was the exit to the outside, and if you made a sharp turn right next door was the Barber Shop, the Saloon, that had a pool table. One day after grandmother and I had finished her cheese run for the day, she and I were on our way home when she invited me to go for a Tommy ice cream bar; after we picked up our Tommy bars and were on our way home when, I finished my ice cream bar, I looked at the stick, my stick had some writing on it. I showed it to grandma, she had a smile on her face as she looked up at me and told me. "You just won a free Tommy Bar." We turned and went back to the ice parlor and received my free Tommy. Back on our way home, I finished and once again I had a stick with the same writing on it. Once again, we turned around for our price, this time we ate it on the spot to make sure we did not have to return, one sweet memory. All of Madrid's activities were handled by the 'Madrid Employee's Club'. Every holiday whether the 4th of July, Easter Sunday, New Year, along with the Christmas celebration was handled by them. This was what made the town of Madrid so famous back in the pre-forty', and of course, baseball was the most thought of because of the night lights where many night games were played. Now, I will say something about Mr. Oscar Huber who was the Superintendent of the town of Madrid; I was told that he was a Jewish Christian.

Chapter 5
Memories of a Cowboy

Now I will take you in a journey with my memories of my father's family life in Madrid as told to me by my father. My grandparents on the Padilla side were wealthy ranchers back in time when they started; they lived in Las Vegas, New Mexico. My father was their only child, who was born there in Las Vegas New Mexico in the year 1900'. I do not know much about my father's younger life, except what my father has told me. He started telling me about his memories as a teenager by saying, that after he had finished his schooling, the depression hit them very hard, so the cow hands had to be laid off and his education was placed on hold, he became a cattle herd tender at the family ranch, his future education was placed aside. World 1 war was at hand from July 1914 on to November 11, 1918. Father had just turned of age and knowing that he was going to be drafted he talked it over with grandma and grand Pa and decided to go join the army. Not knowing that the war had ended, he went to the Army Enlisting Center in Las Vegas; when he entered, he noticed how happy the people were acting. He stood in the enlisting line and wondered why everyone was so happy, when his turn in line came up, the clerk asked him if he could help him. Father told him that he was there to volunteer in the army for he knew that he was going to be inducted soon. The military clerk then told him with a big smile on his face, "You do not have to volunteer son; the war was over three days ago." Father told me that he just turned around and walked out.

When he got home, he told my grandparents that the war was over, and he did not have to join; it became one happy moment for them. In a short time, things went back to normal. Father loved horses and learned to break horses there at the ranch, and on to the local county fairs. As time went on, he became champion as a bronco-busting cowboy, until one day he met his match with a horse that refused to be ridden. They were in a physical action; when the stallion somehow tripped and fell against a wall, the stallion dropped, he broke his hip with my father still in the saddle and down they went; father was trapped and got both legs broken and from then on, he was unable to ride broncos again. As for the horse? Father told me the Stallion had to be shot on the spot and carried away. Some two years went by, and father was able to walk once again. His Love for the rodeo was still deep in his mind knowing that he could never ride again. He took up pistol target shooting and quick draw in the back of their house. One day, father was practicing his shooting in the backyard, when an old friend I will call Jack came by. He stood watching my father at work with the pistol; he had to say something, as he spoke up saying, "Boy, Gabe, you're good, you ever thought about competition at the rodeo." Papa walked up to Jack and shook his hand, replying. "Are you crazy?" Jack replied, "No, no, I know what I'm looking at, what do you say Gabe? I'll place your name on the lineup next month." It did not take much to convince my father. In time he became a sharpshooter putting on shows and competitions locally. He became so good that he became an exhibition artist with the handgun; able to hit a silver dollar size token shooting from the hip at some 30 feet. He became noticed by the Hollywood movie industry and was asked if he would like to become a movie star cowboy; but that would be an insult to men in a man's world, for you may be thought of as a sissy. That was my father's life when he was a young man, I truly remember him telling me all this as if it was only yesterday. The letters he had received from the movies studios were saved by him for an unknown reason, I was so glad he did. All those memories will always be in my mind and my heart. He had quite a few letters; from the many different movie studies such as, MGM, Columbia, Fox, Universal, Paramount Studios, and many others. Why the memory that became so memorable to me were the logos and the symbols on the headings of all the letterheads that I saw, all in color. You still see them in the marquee and in the beginning of all the old movies. All this only shows me how ignorant people were back then when an opportunity like that that only comes once in a lifetime was looked down on as nonsense, not knowing what the entertainment industry would become in the future. I am so glad he did not do that, otherwise I would not be here sitting and writing this manuscript today. All the letters were lost when we moved to California in 1942 due to the (WW2) World War Two action. To this day, I so miss the things that were left behind and amongst them were the letters from the many studios in Hollywood sent to my father. The family were cattle ranchers and were well-to-do, but when the depression hit, things, became extremely hard, and much was lost within the family's life; they became somewhat in poverty almost penniless with only the few cattle and the clothes on their backs. The only thing they could depend on was the sale of the cheese grandma would make that she sold from door to door. My grandma Mary (Padilla) was a professional at making cheese. The day would start at sunrise with milking off the cows, churning the milk in a large container then cooked on a wood stove, then separate the cream and curd, after the process she would place the curd into cheesecloth to squeeze out the liquid, she then would place the curd into a one-pound Hills Brothers coffee cans as a mold to shape the cheese to cure into round blocks and of to market at 25 cents each. She made different types of cheese products. I remember watching her make cheese and filling orders for her customers. Survival had become a necessity to everyone around. The Indian people were hit the hardest; they started taking cows from my grandfather's ranch at night for food. The behaving of the dogs barking was understood, grandpa would fire a shot in the air to scare the robbers away for he knew what was going on; this went on for a while; my grandfather was losing many cows, so he decided to sell or trade the cattle and replace them with goats knowing the native American would not eat goat meat. By now you know that my grandmother Mary was a professional at making cheese products, now making goat cheese became her goal. This was one of the ways she helped made a living with a trade given to her by her mother, my great grandmother Chanette Newman, who's family lived in Detroit Michigan where my grandmother was born; as far as I recall she had two brothers, I do not remember meeting them other than through pictures and letters grandma and father received preaortic. Their names were, Uncle Benito Newman, and Uncle, Louis Newman, better known as Kid Newman. He became the world batten-weight boxing Champion in his heyday. Much later in his life, he became known for the Newman Gyms in different cities here in America to this day.

His history and his wealth are unknown to me and lost in time. The time had come for Grandfather Padilla to move away from the area due to the goats' gracing habits. Goats are known for destroying the land due to their eating habits, for they would eat everything in sight, and this left the family with many difficulties and conflicts with the other farmers. My grandfather had to move. He had a brother named Miguel who lived in that small community called Waldo quite a few miles from Las-Vegas. Waldo had become a coal transferring station coming from the town of Madrid for The Atchison, Topeka, and Santa Fe Railroad Company. Where my uncle Miguel worked. The nearest store was about two or three miles away in a little town called Los-Cerrillos; this is the town that had a train station that was the main line from the east to Albuquerque and on to the Santa Fe, from there to the west coast; this was the same line that brought me and my family to California, in 1942. It was hard for them to find a place with open land where they could grace and corral the goats. My grandfather's brother, Uncle Miguel, suggested a place near the Madrid arroyo where they could walk a mile or so into town for their needs and grandpa could work in the coal mines if needed. It is unknown to me how or when they arrive to the north end of the Madrid territory where they homestead. It was told to me by my grandma that someone in the family had passed on who had three children that were left orphaned, the lady had one son who was maned Thomas he was a young boy of thirteen years of age left alone with no one to take care of him or his two sisters; so, grandma adopted Thomas; Thomas became the goat tender at the ranch; he would take the goats gracing out in the fields every day and help milk the goats so grandma could make the cheese to sale daily. By now she had made many customers. As for my father, he moved on and became a cattle cowboy herding cattle for one of the largest ranchers in Utah. A story that comes to mind is one my father told me about his life as a cowboy there in Utah. he started by telling me that he had been working for over a year with a Utah cattle rancher. One day he was told to go on a cattle drive with some two hundred cows from Utah to Texas that would take quite a few days on the trail. Father had become overseer over the working crew, he had four Chinese workers along with them; one was a cook and the other three were the cook's helpers, those were the folks who taught my father to speak the Cantonese Chinese one of the several languages my father could speak fluently. After they delivered the cattle, they were paid, and now it was time for relaxing. The gang ended up in a local saloon that had the longest serving bar ever seen by any of them. As they were having a few drinks one of the local men heard the Utah boys bragging about my father being a sharpshooter, they were trying to get him to put on a show to make a few bucks betting on the side. In the crowd was a big fellow that heard them talking and bragging about father being a sharpshooter, he walked over to where my father was drinking his beer and started a ruffle over what he had heard about my father being a so-called a great sharpshooter with the handgun. Father told me that he tried to ignore the man, but the man became very loud and out of hand insulting and cursing him. At that time, the room became silent as the man walked on to the upset end of the bar some thirty feet give or take; the locals knew what this man had in mind when he would walk and flared his coat back to expose his 44, he was known for his temper's ways, saying with a loud voice, "It's time for you to proof how bad you are with that little toy you have strapped around your skinning ass." Father never carried a heavy pistol, only the pistol that was made especially for him by the rodeo organization back home. He only used it in exhibitions at the rodeos or to kill snakes, he would use a heavier hollow point load on the trail in case of wolfs; it was a special made 38 caliber pistol that was well balanced; as for the other fellow, he had a 44 caliber twice as large as that of my father's, so called, a toy pistol. Everyone moved away from the center laughing and cheering the big fellow on knowing what was about to happened, as the man reached to draw his 44, father had his in motion and shot him. He told me that he did not try to kill the man, as far as he knew he aimed for the shoulder of the man's shooting arm in the hope the man would never be able to use his shooting arm again. That was my father's intention. Everyone gathered around the local man who was known to them as Big Jim. This gave time for my father to tell his men that it was time to get out of town fast, and to get back to the campsite and get the wagons and the men ready to move out pronto. The wagons had already been loaded that morning for they were to leave the following day. All that was needed was for the men to hook up the horses and within a half hour the horses were ready. They got on the trail heading back to Utah. It was a rather dark night when they left not knowing if the towns men would come looking for them at sunrise. The area was unknown to them, and it was decided by my father to get off the main trail. Although it was rather dark, the men took time to dust off the wagon tracks for a good mile from the main road and on to their new destination home, the trail was extremely rigid but, they went without an incident. After all those years, father still had that incident deep in his mind, every time he got tipsy, he would tell me about the man he had shot not knowing if the man had died or not. The memories of that incident were burned deep in my father's mind that never left him. After some years as a cowboy, he returned home to the ranch in Madrid and became a coal miner. Somewhere in time he met and married my mother.

Chapter 6
Somewhere in Time

Now back to my childhood. The early life of my father and mother together was never spoken of, except that my mother had a total of five children. The plague of the 20's and the 30's came upon the land, and took three of my mother's siblings, my two little sisters. Antoinette, Josephine, and my older brother John Anthony. The only two that were left were my sister Frances and me. The first home I remember is the little white house near the arroyo. If you remember that is where I was introduced to eating Chile by my father. It is extremely hard to remember the exact dates or age as I go on with my story. As time passes on, I remember we moved to a large rustic house at the west end of town. There were not many friends around to play with I remember two brothers that lived about the distance of a half block just below the road in front of our house. We would play cowboys and bandits, I always wanted to be the Lone Ranger and my horse silver was an old broom stick. One of the boys I played with was named Pablo he had a little brother name was Nut-tea he was always the bad guy, poor little guy he was always the one who got shot or put in jail. As for my sister, she walked to school across the arroyo every day. Once again, father was deciding to move; by now you are probably wondering why we moved so much? Well! Father wanted us to live in a better area; every time someone would leave or move, he would put a bid for the house, knowing that he would move us to a better location. Now, about this new place that we were living in, it was a nice house; it had a double seated outhouse. The only plumbing we had back then was a water pump up a way that one had to bring the water in buckets; only the houses on Main Street had indoor plumbing. Father was not satisfied with this house. One day he came in from work with a smile on his face and gathered all of us to tell the good news. He said, "I was talking with a fellow worker today, he brought up about the house where they lived and went on talking to me about having four kids and not having separation between the kids, for he had two boys and two girls." They want on talking. Father liked the place where the man was living at. As they were talking father came up with an idea, so he asked the man if maybe they could exchange houses. It did not take long for the man to reply, saying, "I will talk it over with my wife, I am sure she will be very happy." After the exchanging, things became better. The one-bedroom house had a porch that father converted into a bedroom where my sister and I slept. The backyard was on the hillside that had four fruit trees and a small garden very unusual in a coal mining town, mother loved it. Above the garden is where the outhouse was. On this hill is where I played and ventured with my activity; this was where I had a great time playing and flying my kite, also hiking to the top of the hill; from there I could see all of Madrid. The Morgan mine was to my far left, and so was the road that went to the Cemetery where my sisters and my brother lay to rest on the flat part of the hill; just a distance below was, The Morgan coal dump station where the coal was cleaned and separated and shipped to Los-Cerrillos; and looking to my right was the Jones and the Lamb mines. Across from where we lived one could see the ballpark and the grandstand, they were straight ahead in the distances on the opposite side of the valley, so was the schoolhouse. On Front Street was a large hotel called Hotel Number 9 this is where the visitors stayed; and on the south end of Front Street to the far right is where the smokestacks of the power plant that made the electricity that powered the town. Farther down was the Breaker, very noisy and very loud, this is where the breaking of the large rocks of coal were broken down to size, and then sent off to market. From this house my sister and I walked to school every day, and just across the arroyo was the trail that went up to the schoolhouse, and next to the school was the start of Main Street, called Front Street. The first house was the house where the school principal Mr. Crider lived; he was a big man; he had a son named Terry who became my best friend. After school he would invite me to go play with him in his backyard, he had many toys that a boy like me could only imagine; he had dump trucks, cars and houses we would make our own towns. Mother approved of me coming late from school knowing where I was. Mr. Crider was also the manager of the auditorium and movie theater there in town. I had just entered the third grade. One day the teacher was called out, when she returned, she told me that Mr. Crider wanted to talk to me. I wonder what he wanted. As I entered the office, he asked me to sit down. He then, without hesitation looking straight into my eyes, asked me if I had taken the theater money bag from his house. He was serious; I never felt as frightful as I did at that very moment. He asked me again, "Did you take the money bag with $37.50 from my desktop at my home? Terry told me that you and he went in the house to get some toys, he also told me he left you waiting while he used the bathroom." All I did while waiting for him was just look at all the toys he had. Mr. Crider continued saying, "Now! I know you took that money, for no one else had been in the house other than you and Terry." All I could do was wimpier with fear and tears in my eyes. He said, "I will give you time to bring that money back; now go back to your room I will talk with you later." I did not even know what money was, all I ever had was a penny or maybe a dime at the most; I walked back to my room, no one said a word as to why I was called to go see Mr. Crider. It was lunch time and I stayed to myself, wondering how all this happened and what would I tell my mother and father? The bell rang I went back to the room drying the tears in my eyes. A while had passed by, and once again, I was called to the office. As I entered, I was very frightful and crying telling Mr. Crider that I did not take the money bag. He walked up to me and placed his hands on my shoulders, and I not knowing and with much fear if he was going to spank me; he looked at me and with a softer voice he said. "Sit, down son," he posed as he spoke softly, "I have an apology to make to you I made a very bad mistake accusing you of taking the money, I went home for lunch and looked around again, as I looked up at the cabinet above my desk I remembered that, that's where I had placed the money bag, and not remembering where I had placed it; I feel so embarrassed; please forgive me; I have a little gift for you for my mishap with my apology please forgive me." I just sat there sobbing, in his hand, he was holding a black wallet; he then handed it to me; I was afraid to take it, he then told me not to be afraid; I slowly took the wallet as he said, "Open it!" I unfolded the wallet and to my surprise, a paper dollar bill was in it; paper money was very unusual other than scrip that was used by company workers to shop at the store. With fear, I took the wallet. Before he excused me, he gave me a note to give my parents explaining the mistake he had made with his apology. It left me with a fear of a spanking when papa got home. I walked back to my room, and no one seemed to have missed me and things were somewhat back to normal. Now I was looking forward to explaining to my parents the story. As for Terry? He was still my friend, but I never played at his house ever again. One day, after school let out, I was at the front of the schoolyard, I had my homework paper in my hand, when a gust of wind blew my homework paper right out of my hand. The paper flew across the street, I ran up the cement steps that led to the sidewalk just above the front of the school and across the street. I ran after my school paper; when I reached where the paper had landed at the bottom of the hillside, I bent over to pick it up my paper, and right in front of me was a one-dollar bill in the weeds, as I bent over to pick it up I looked around I saw no one; I was on my way up, and just a few feet farther was another dollar bill laying in the weeds; I went and pick it up, and again another short distance in front of me was a third dollar bill laying on the weedy ground. Three one-dollar bills unknown how they got there! It had to do something with the wind that was blowing so hard that day. I told no one till I got home and told mama; she quizzed me, and I finally convinced her. Another incident happened to me there at the school; some friends of the family had a boy named David and a daughter named Sally; Sally was in my class and an exceptionally good friend of mine but her brother who was in a higher grade was a bully and always picking on me. One day after school, I was on my way to the back of the school where the downhill trail home was, I never got to the trail, he saw me and started running towards me I started running in the opposite direction from the trail home I ran across the ballpark to the area where the so-called Hollywood homes were; at the end of the street was where uncle Victor lived; I had only one way to go, that was the downslope at the end of the home track. The slope was a good forty feet and a steep drop; this is where many kids used to slide down on cardboard, I never stopped running, I leaped, and in four large steps I made it to the bottom thank God it was soft dirt, David didn't stop he kept on coming after me, it took him a bit longer to reach the bottom I was quite a ways ahead of him; I ran across the arroyo on to the street where my home was some three blocks away; I remember running and crying yelling, "mama, mama David is after me." He stopped about three blocks away; he must have heard me yelling for my mother. After that, I do not remember what my mother said to me, only that she would have a talk with Dave's mother. After that, Dave stayed away from me. Another memory comes to me, this happened back when I was about four give or take, I do not remember what house we were living in at that time, when a family known to my folks were on their way back to their home to a town called Galisteo a few miles north; it so happened that the lady's time to give birth was at hand; they were welcomed by my parents. I and their little girl were told to go out and play; we went to the back of the house to play. A bit later the little girl had to go pee pee, and so did I. Being at an innocent age, we decided to go under the porch, we started to pee-pee when I noticed that I was standing, and she had to squat? I stared with curiosity and took notice as to why we were different and why I had a long thing and hers was missing! I just did not know why hers was missing, and after looking we touched each other so innocently; with our childishly ways we then decided to make one like mine for her; I made it out of our pee-pee mud, I rolled the mud with my hand, and she took it and placed it on her private part. We were laughing and having a great time, when her grandmother approached; she screamed out at us saying, "What are you two doing?" We did not know, the only thing that came to my mind as to what we were doing wrong was, that pee mud was stinky and nasty to play with. She went on saying with a loud voice, "If I catch you doing this again, I will tell your parents and you will be spanked, and I will be keeping my eyes on you". What happened after that? I do not remember. But I never thought of playing like that again.

Chapter 7
Madrid, December 7, California

Madrid was a unique and pleasant town, it was well known for the Fourth of July celebrations, the Easter hunt and parades, and the most famous of all was the Christmas celebration and decorations. Madrid was nestled between surrounding hills and down to a narrow valley below; it had a railroad that would carry the mined coal to Waldo, and on to Los Cerrillos where the main Santa Fe transferring line was and sent to market. Sometime around mid-November the town started the Christmas decorations. La Mocha, or shorty, as the Santa Fe locomotive # 769 was called, arrived loaded with many Christmas trees; the smell of Christmas filled the air. A tree was delivered to every house as usual and all were wired with many colored light bulbs, red, blue, orange, yellow, white, and green. Every Christmas, many visitors came from many parts around to see this wonderland. Which brings another episode to mine? Christmas time in Madrid. I mentioned earlier the superintendent of Madrid, was Mr. Oscar Huber, thought to be a Jewish Christian, who believed in the Nativity that he displayed as you enter Front Street from the north/east side just past the school: there in full-size figures were where the manger scene lay, with life animals, two donkeys maybe two or three sheep, a couple of goats, a cow and bull and a life-size manger setting, I remember how impressive it was. Coming from Los Cerrillos on the east side to the right, was the ballpark, this is where the most spectacular fairyland you could ever imagine came to life, and it was called Toyland. Walt Disney eat your heart out; this must be where Walt Disney got his ideas. In the park is where all the fairyland characters came to life, they stood so high that they had to be placed in place with a Crane. Let us start with the characters mentioned in the fairytale books that come to mind. The cow jumped over the moon, The old woman who lived in a shoe, Jack and the Beanstalk, Mary had a little lamb, Jack jumped over the candle stick, the Three Little Pigs, and Humpy Dumpty, Micky Mouse, Minnie Mouse, and his three nephews, Jack and Jill walking up the hill. Every fairy tale character one can imagine came to life. The last image I remember that was placed in the park around 1940, was little boy Blue standing on a post-up high playing his trumpet, three blue musical notes would display from his trumpet. All scenes were in a motional movement, it was a most imaginable enjoyment for children of all ages in this magical land of fairy tales come true. There was also a small rail locomotive that traveled around the playground that the children would ride free on Christmas day. Every house had a well-lit Christmas tree and many decorated lights throughout the main street and throughout the whole town. At both entrances when entering Madrid, were a welcome arch, one on the North end and the other on the South end they displayed a glowing welcome with a Merry Christmas in the center of the arches. Now let us go to the south side of town, coming in from Albuquerque. If my memory serves me right, as you enter Madrid, just up away from the welcome arch lay a display on the side of the hill that represents a choirboys' scene, with twelve boys, six on one side, Jesus on the cross in the center, and the other six boys on the opposite side of the cross. The scene had a public address system, the choirboys would move their mouths up and down in motion as if they were singing, somewhat realistic. I remember the local folks talking about an incident that happened one night at this site. Mr. Huber had hired a local Mexican man to run the sound system on the choir display nightly. The story goes that, one night the man got a little tipsy, well—drunk, and decided to play Mexican music. The PA system sounded very loudly; and the neighbors were wondering where the loud music was coming from; and oh, yes! The choirboys were singing, "Ayaan El Rancho Grande" And other Mexican songs. This became the talk of the town; unknown as to what happened to the man after that? Following the road into town was the main street, it called it Front Street. This was the area where most of the well-to-do lived. The upper street was called Back Street. These were the only two main streets in the town; just above Back Street on the hill site was a display of the City of Bethlehem; it was a good square city block in length if not longer, and the dwellings were built in a realistic size. Just above the city was the 14 ft. Star of Bethlehem glowing so brightly and could be seen from afar and throughout the town. On the same hill side were the three kings traveling to Bethlehem, they were following the North Star in search of the king of kings, Jesus the Christ as told to them by an angel. One more memory. At the highest hill in Madrid just above The Breaker, Mr. Huber had a huge Christmas tree made up of some 50 or more Christmas trees placed together into one huge tree, with hundreds of color lights, the tree could be seen from many miles around as far as Santa Fe. I could go on, but it is time for me to continue with my story. December 7, 1941 was the last time the light of

Christmas shined in Madrid. Madrid had to turn off the light due to the World War Two conflict. That day December seven, nineteen forty-one. The radio became a voice of terror. Walter Winchell was a newspaper and radio commentator; his voice was heard on the local radio, K. G. G. M., and in many other radio stations. He started his newscast by saying, "Good evening Mr. and Mrs. America, today on this very day, December 07, 1941, I come with a heavy heart, for today America has declared war with Japan," and so on? My sister and I being youngsters did not understand what this was all about. Fear set in and father had to try to explain to us without scaring us. A few days later, father came home with some news that some government man had come to have a talk with the miners, saying that help was needed to build war ships and that the government would pay their passage and a place to stay until they could pay on their own, this was offered to anyone who would volunteer to work in the in the shipyards in the San Francisco Bay area, and Richmond California across the bay. Things became quiet and unknowingly what was to happen, as to what answer would come from mother if father decided to go. This would be a departure in the family that has never been thought off. Mother, and father talked things over with Grandma and Grandpa Padilla with tear-filled eyes and as they talked it over and it was decided that it would be better to get away from the present poverty. Some two weeks later came the day for everyone to gather at the front of the general store where everyone was to bid farewell to those who volunteered to work in the shipyards in California; there were many tears and waving goodbyes as the brown army bus pulled away with their loved ones aboard. This left my mother in such sorrow for the family had never been separated before. Every night after she placed us to bed, she would get on her knees and sobbing with tear-filled eyes as she prayed for comfort reading with her Spanish bible in her hands; (I still have one of her Spanish bibles.) My sister and I could hear her praying knowing that her heart was sad over the departure of father. I would cover my head under my pillow with fear that mother and my sister would hear me sobbing. Cousin Lupe was staying with us he also was working in the mines and in fear of being drafted into the military but, it so happened those miners were exempted from the draft due to the need for coal in the military and fear of lung disease from the coal fumes, luck was with him, he was exempt from the draft. The only sound that was heard about was the noisy Breaker in the distance for the town had fallen asleep. No Christmas lights, no Christmas music. Cousin Lupe became the man of the house, he took over the monthly rental payment for the house. Time went on, which comes to mind. One day, Cousin Lupe was invited to a party with the guys he was asked to bring his 78 records collections with him; sometime late in the night, he was on his way home a bit tipsy with his record collection in hand. He told me he had fallen, and all his records were demolished and irreplaceable. Next day, he took me and show where he had fallen; sure, enough one Million fragments all over the road, and with much laughter we walked on home. We resided there for some three-month after father had left. mother had to sell many of the precious things she had for many years in order to raise enough money to go to where father was, somewhere in the San Francisco Bay California. Many things had to be left behind, the one thing that is most embedded in my memories were the letters my father had saved from the many Hollywood studios that were sent to him to be a cowboy actor in the movies. The day had come, it was time to say farewell to Grandma and Grandpa Padilla and everyone else we knew; many tears were shed. Cousin Lupe drove us to Los Cerrillos where we took the Santa Fe train to Albuquerque where we were transferred to the passenger train going to a place called Oakland California. Now, remembering what the train looked like to me as I stood there staring in suspense? There were two very large engines from the Santa Fe railway, they were called 4-8-4. We walked alongside them to get to our car, and I remember as I stood staring at the wheels, they were so Hugh well over six feet or more. What an amazing site for a young child to look at; the only trains I knew of was a toy train my friend Terry had, not realizing how large a real train was. The length of the whole train was 28 passenger cars plus the two 4-8-4 engines along with their huge water tanks hooked behind each engine. We had to walk quite a long way to get to our passenger car, this was where the lower-class passenger cars were. As we entered our car, I saw many men dressed in white uniforms and white caps, yes! They were Sailors, unknown to me what a Sailor was? The train was coming from the East coast to the west coast for the men to be deployed to duty at The San Francisco Naval base called Treasure Island. We were told to sit at the front of the car, we were the only civilians in that car for mama could not afford for a luxurious compartment, so we were placed on one of rear passenger car. My mother, my sister Frances, and I with a bunch of men in white uniforms; unknown to me what a sailor was. We were the only three civilians in that car, everyone else were sailors; and every one of them treated me and my sister so wonderful; one sailor bought me and my sister an apple, he could see that my sister and I, all we could do was look and drool when the porter had passed us by, one of the sailor knew mama had no money to buy an apple, those apples cost 25 cents each, it was amazing how expensive an apple cost on that train, but they were big apples. So, done we thanked the Sailor, he had a nice smile on his face. Now, another exerts happened on the train, it was getting late, and we were sleepy, we were leaning on mother, for mother could not pay for a pillow or a blanket, I remember how cold it was; when one of the sailor saw this, he asks the potter to bring us a pillow and something to cover us with and that he would pay for it. Those sailors treated us so great that I still pray with much thankfulness for all those sailors that were in that train car with us who serviced our country in that World War Two action, they will never be forgotten deep in my heart. We traveled all night. The next day, we arrived in a place called Phoenix, Arizona, the stop was short, and on to Bakers Field California, then on to Fresno, Modesto, Stockton, Martinez, and on to Richmond California, from there, to the final stop at the Oakland train station, I believe it was on 26th. Street, that was the end of the line. From there the train went to the West Oakland train yard on First Street, just across was the Alameda estuary where the U S Army and the Naval Air Base were. From there, the sailors were to be deployed to Treasure Island and on to their destination, Godspeed.

Chapter 8
Settling in California From 606 to 5400 - 2B

One of my most memorable moments I remember. As we approached the San Francisco Bay coming into what is called, point Pinole my sister and I were looking out the window and to our surprise we saw the San Francisco Bay not knowing what we were looking at, I remember me yelling out! 'Look mama it's the Ocean!" Just then all the sailors raced to the windows with amazement, none of us knew what a bay was, to us it was the ocean. As we moved on, coming into the North Richmond Bay, just across the bay were a couple of islands not known to us that one was San Quintain and the other, was Angel Island. Beyond the horizon was the famous Golden Gate bridge unknown to many of us on the train. All the coastal mountains were covered with many huge balloons all along the horizon, also unknown to us what they were, until one of the sailors explained to us what they were and what there for. He said that they were there to protect the coast of incoming enemy air crafts. This sounded somewhat spooky to me, as he went on explaining that that was the reason why no enemy would dare attempt to attack our shores. Yes, that made me feel somewhat safer now on our arrival at Oakland, I vaguely remember a yellow cab taking us to a friend's place that had come from back home sometime earlier. They lived at 606 Caster St. From there I do not remember how we got to San

Francisco to where my father lived. He lived 981 McAlister St. in a dormitory with other men. Father was talking with the friend that came with us about not having a place for us to live yet. The man then said he would rent the basement section where he lived in Oakland. Father took the day off to help us move in at 606 Castro St. It was a rather dumpy place, but it became home. The next morning, I woke up with many etching bumps all over my body and so did my folks; not knowing what a blood-sucking flea was, my parents thought it may be bed bugs. Dad made a complaint to the man who lived upstairs. The man told him that they were flea bites and that they were common, he sprayed the house, we had to stay outside for a long while, while the house was airing out, hoping this would rid the flea invasion. Well, it worked for a while. It was hard to get used to this filthy way of living. Another excerpt comes to mind, that was the rat infestation that roamed all night long, we could hear them. I remember father buying a loaf of bread he left on the counter, next morning at breakfast, mother went to pick up the loaf to set on the table; as she grabbed the loaf, to her surprise all she got was the bread rapper full of air. After father looked at the bread rapper, there was a small hole on the back of it; it was so amazing how a mouse took all the bread out and left the bread rapper standing empty. One evening, about nine O' o'clock, the sirens went off and everything went on a black-out alert, and this brought fear to all of us. Just across the estuary was the Alameda Naval Air Base, from there the fighter planes flew over the houses, their engines were very loud; many of the neighbors were outside looking in wonderment and fear. It took well over half an hour when the All-clear sign blasted off. The planes returned to base. As time went on, Father had been waiting for an opening on what was called a war housing apartment in Richmond California. After six months, father was able to get a war housing apartment in South Richmond bordering El Cerrito California, just a short way from our apartment was what was called Highway 40 back then and it connected to San Pablo Avenue known to be the longest avenue ever, well over 23 miles, it ran from 14th. And Broadway Ave. in Oakland all the way to the city of Crockett. Highway 40 is now called the Interstate, I-80, different from the old highway 40 of yesterday. We were so glad to move away from 606 Castro Street. The next day, we left early morning with what little baggage we had, we took a trolly car to the Ashby Avenue Station, at the San Pablo Avenue terminal in Berkeley; that was the end line for the trolley car service to downtown Oakland; from there we took the Key System bus; there were two different buses going to Richmond, the 72 M. and the 72 P, the M. stood for McDonald Ave. and P. for Potrero Ave. We took the 72 M to 10th. And McDonald Avenue. Father asked the bus driver that we were looking for Cutting Boulevard where the housing authority was. He told father we had to get off at 10th. St. and go south. We got off the bus, not knowing which way to go; father ask a man on the street for direction, the man told papa that he had to walk up 10th street for about a half mile as he pointed south; then we had to walk a few blocks up Cutting Boulevard to 16th St. and assured father that we could not miss it. We were on our way, my father, my mother, my sister, and yours truly. We reached Cutting Boulevard and on to 16th St.; sure, enough there it was. As we entered the office, Father walked up to the window and filled in all the information needed for a two-bedroom furnished apartment. The man told us to wait a few minutes. It did not take him long. When he returned, he walked up to us with a handful of blankets, four pillows, he said it was part of furnishing, he also gave father a paper showing how to get to our destination. He said that our address was 5400 Jefferson Avenue apt. 2 B. We looked at each other with smiling faces. We started walking east from 16th St.; halfway we passed an area called The Easter Hill apartments on passed 23rd. St. and about seven more blocks and across the tracks to Carlson Blvd where we turned right at Carlson; then we walked maybe half a mile to a street called Potaro Avenue, from there maybe 5 more blocks on to the beginning of Jefferson Avenue. Jefferson Ave. was a long street that went all the way to San Pablo Ave. before the freeway came about; we walked on. We reached some light brown colored Apartments but, they did not match the address on the paper father had. As we walked on about three more blocks more, we reached an area that had a large building called, Housing Authority Recreation Center Building, and just beyond we could see the apartments, they were different, better looking and more modern, they were white with green trim and the house numbers were looking better; wouldn't you know it! It had to be the last apartment on Jefferson Avenue near highway 40. We never intended to walk that far but not having a car, we walked, and it became a joy. The apartments had 12 good-sized living quarters and two single units, one on each end of the apartment. As we entered the apartment it was fully furnished, what a comfort. My sister and I sat on the couch and papa sat on the armchair. Mama took a walk looking with such amazement at this new world to come. In the back of the apartments was a washhouse, a cloth-line, a play yard, with 2 swings', titter-tatter, marry-ground, and a sand box. This was the best babysitter of that time. It was late summer in 1942 when we saddled at 5400 Jefferson Avenue apt. 2 B. Most people were shipyard workers, and the majority came from Oklahoma, Texas, Missouri, Arkansas and New Mexico. Which I recall a song from back in the 40th.' It was called, 'Dear Okie'. (The song goes:) "Oh dear Okie if you see Arkie tell him Tax has a job for him out in Califor-nie, just a picking up prunes squeezing oil out of olives." (You can look this song up in the NET. It is a blast.) Meanwhile, my memories go on. I made a few friends, there were two brothers that come to mind, one was named Ross and his older was called A. J. their last name was Griffin. A. J. was one of those overweight smart-ass bullies, with a vulgar mouth. He was a couple years older than me and his brother. One day we were playing at the playground, A. J. tied a good size rock to a rope and started swinging it, around and around went the rope it was some 15 feet long; his brother and I were watching, when, the rock came flying off the end of the rope. Of all the open air around in that circle that darn rock picked me and landed right on the back of my head, OUCH, it is a wonder it did not knock me out but, I did see many bright stars. The boys took me home to our apartment; everything turned out well, except for a huge knot and a bloody neck. It was there that started my schooling where I left off back home in the third grade. The school was, and still is called Stege Elementary School, on School Avenue in South Richmond. It amazed me that I had learned my fractions in the third grade back home and here at Stege they did not start teaching fractions until I was in the 6th grade. That is how far back the schooling was in California back then. After I finished grade school, I went to Long

Fellow Junior High School just off 23rd Street a short way from McDonald Avenue. Across was the Gray Hound bus station and a motorcycle shop. My birthday was coming up and my sister planned a birthday party for me, it was my 12th. Birthday that year. We did not really know what a real birthday party was like back then; but it turned out great. Another great memory there at the Long Fellow junior high; we were playing softball that day, the field was a good square block long facing 23rd. street, I was up at bat and I saw a man watching the game leaning on the fence a little past the third base, he was wearing a hat, and joking, I told the guys, "see that man over there? I'm going to knock his hat off," of course the gang was laughing at me, now, you won't believe this one, I hit the ball and sure as I'm sitting here writing this novel, God is my witness, the ball flew right at the man, he ducked down and on his way down my ball hit knocked his hat off, thank God the ball didn't hit him, he busted out laughing and so did the kids and the coach, I became the man of the year. Back then, big band music was the thing, Harry James was a great trumpet player and I fell in love with the trumpet so I took up music at school only to find that all the trumpets were taken, back then the school had free use of the instrument's for the students to use, all the trumpet were taken so the music teacher used the excuse that I had the lips for the trombone, I took the trombone for a half-semester that I was stuck with, so I gave it up; one big mistake. I graduated from the 9th grade and on to El Cerrito High School where I graduated in 1952. Back in my teenage years I was different than most kids, I was quiet and spent most of my time listening to adventurous serials on the radio, I would come home from school and do my chores around the house, and when finished, it was time to go on to my dream world with my radio adventures like the Long Ranger, Superman, Jack Armstrong, and so forth; after supper it was my parent's turn with the radio. Every Saturday evening, a program came on at eight o'clock called 'The Harry Owens, and His Royal Hawaiian show' direct from Hawaii; this is where I was blessed with a dream for the steel guitar. A couple of blocks up, lived a young friend who had a traditional cheap Gena Autry guitar that was broken at the neck, he traded with me for something, I cannot remember what, but we made the trade, I took it home and asked my father if he would fix it for me; so, done. Back then in the forties, the Hawaiian guitar became very popular. The music shops would lend you a steel guitar and if you would take steel guitar lessons, and after one year of schooling, the guitar was yours, this sounded good except for one thing, my parents could not afford for me to continue taking lessons after six lessons, I had too quit. One day I was looking through a Montgomery Ward's catalog in the guitar section and what a blessing, they had a kit that you could convert your regular guitar into a Hawaiian steel guitar; wow, I had my father to order the kit, I couldn't wait; a week passed no package; I came home from school one day, and on the coffee table was a package from Wards I knew the kit arrived; I wanted to open it but, mama said you better wait till your father comes home. Talking about time going slow that clock on the end table seemed to have stopped. After what I thought was a long wait, I heard someone coming up the steps, I ran to the door, it was father. He came and saw me holding the Ward packet in my hands and a twinkle in my eye, the only thing he did was a short greeting and washing his hands. The time came to open the packet; after removing a few things that were ordered at the very bottom was the kit. The moment came, time for me to open the pack and see what I had received, it was a set of guitar strings, a bridge to raise the strings, one plastic thumb pick, two plastic fingertips, a plastic slide bar, and an E-tuner. By now the guitar neck on my Gena Autry guitar was glued and well set hoping it would not come apart. I placed the strings on very carefully, then I placed the E-tuner to my lips and blew in it following the instructions in the manual on how to tune to the E major tuning. In about three months or so I had the guitar mastered, I could play many tunes. Back in the 40s, country music became incredibly famous. There was, and still is, a place on Market St. called Maple Hall, it was a dance hall back then, and this is where many famous country bands played on the weekends. The band I really liked was Bob Wills and his Texas playboys; when he played there my folks would take me to see them. I would go up as close as I could to see the steel guitar player called Leon McCullough, that is where I learned to play the tune called The Steel Guitar rag, by watching him; it took me about three months to learn that piece. I can still remember Bob Wills saying, "Ah ha Take it away Leon, take away my boy." I caught on very well. I had a friend named Jack Mead who lived nearby, he heard me playing on my home-made steel guitar, he then told me that his mother had an electric steel guitar that she tried to learn but could not catch on, "and maybe she will let you play it." It did not take long; as we arrived at the apartment where he lived, he introduced me to his mother. She showed me her steel guitar it was a six-string Gibson lap steel, well beyond my dreams. I had my picks, and my bar with me itching to put my fingers on that steel guitar. She brought out an amplifier and hooked the steel guitar to it, she strummed across the strings it was somewhat out of tune but what a sound. She finely told me to try it. The first thing I did was to tune it. I played for a while; she asks me what kind of steel guitar I had? Being a bit embarrassed I told her. She motioned for Jack to come with her, Jack and his mother walked into the kitchen and were talking, and I kept playing. When they returned, she told me that I could barrow the guitar and the amp. For a while. It did not take long; Jack and I were on the way to my house with guitar and amp; so accomplished. Jack came over to my house to explain to my folks that his mother had lent me her steel guitar. Some time had passed by, I was playing the steel guitar one warm afternoon, and the window was open as my music felt the air, when a man came to the house and introduced himself and said that he lived in the apartment across the street and heard me playing, he told us that he and his family played country music in El Sobrante at a place called The Horseshoe Club. I played a few country tunes for him; he must have been impressed with my plying for he asked me if I would like to play with them at the Horseshoe Club. I looked up at my father, father looked over at me and that is all it took.

I played with his band for a couple of months and was paid 5 dollars a night Friday and Saturday. Father bought me my own steel guitar it was a called a Supro for $49.00 cheap but nice. I told the man that the guitar and amp I was playing was a loner and I had to return it back to its owner, but that father had bought me my own steel except I did not have an amp. The man told me that I could hook up to his amp that it was no problem. One weekend there at the club while getting ready to play, the band leader was talking with a couple of soldiers and called me over, he introduced me to the two GIs who were telling the boss that they were looking for a lead guitar player, for they were losing their lead player that he was being deployed (transferred) elsewhere, and if he knew any lead guitar player around. The boss told them about me and that I was a good lead player on the steel guitar; that is all it took I picked my steel guitar left with them to a new experience. That was the chance of a lifetime for me, from then on this was my new challenge that started at a place called The Trio Club in El Sobrante on the Dam Road, I made more money and became well known. The GIs would pick me up and bring me home. My father was so proud he bought me a double-neck Fender. I had just turned 17 years of age. One night on our 15-minute break, I was sitting in a room at the back of the bar for I was not of age to stay in the main part of the club; that night I was sitting by myself drinking a 7up when I looked up leaning against the wall were three quarter slot machines; no one was around, just me and the slot machines; the jukeboxes were somewhat loud, so, I peeked out the door and saw no one, oh yea! I placed the quarter in the slot pulled the handle and to my surprise the bell went off, bingo, it hit, $3.50; and I told no one Time was up and back to work. The many years I played the honkytonks, I never drank I just did not have the stomach for it; mine was the pleasure of playing my steel guitar and see people enjoy dancing and having a good time; to this day I do not drink sprits. Now I will tell you a little story that happened to me at the Trio Club, someone was having a birthday party and many drinks were passed around, mine was 7up that was offered to me one after another; the next day I woke up with a huge throbbing head, so bad I had to go to the emergency hospital on 23rd St. The first thing the doctor asked, "How much did you had to drink last night?" I told the doctor that I did not drink, he looked at me very funny, and he knew I was 17 and underage. I could tell he did not believe me by the way he looked at me; I said, "That's true doctor, I do not drink". The doctor took a blood sample; I had to wait a while. He came back and told me he could not find anything that could have given me a headache. He replied again, "Are you sure you did not drink sprits last night?" I told him, the only thing I drank last night was 7up. He looked at me and smiled and asked, "How much 7up, did you drink?" I replied, "Quite a bit, I play steel-guitar at the Trio club and last night someone had a birthday party and drinks were free, people knew I did not drink so, 7up was my drink." He then smiled and said, "Now I know why, you have so much sugar in your blood, you have a hangover from too much 7up and that's what gave you that huge headache." As bad as I was hurting, I had to laugh along with him. He gave me a pill, and I drove myself home I had a good sleep. After two years or so of playing at the Trio Club, the two GIs were deployed elsewhere; that ended my playing for a while. Although there were many temptations, I never had bad intentions while playing my steel guitar in the many pubs I played, because I just enjoyed what I loved, which was playing my steel guitar for the many folks, many of them came up front just to watch me play and tip me. That was my joy, playing my steel guitar.

Chapter 9
Painful Moments

As for entertainment back in my teen years, going to the movies was a great pastime, Richmond had quite a few theaters starting from First and Mc Donald Ave, was the Rio, the State, the U A, and the Fox, theaters there were another one I believe it was called the Studio, or Balboa? Now going up farther up Mc Donald Ave, beyond 23rd St. was the Up-Town Theater, and on to San Pablo Avenue near Potrero Ave. was where the Vista Theater set, this was the nearest theater to where I lived; not to forget the drive-in theaters, there were three, one was the Rancho drive in (1950), the San Pablo Auto movies (1953), and the Hill-Top drive in (1963). Around 1946 the war apartments were being eliminated and we had to move. It was hard to find a place to live, so we ended on first and Ohio avenue in Richmond in a small raunchy hotel called, The Santa Fe Hotel; we lived on the second floor, just below our apartment was a bar with a jukebox that blasted all night till around two in the morning. It took us a while to get used to it. Next door to the hotel lived a boy about my age that I made friends with, his name was Roberto, he lived there with his grandmother. She was the cook for the fruit pickers in the fruit fields passed the town called Fairfield off highway forty, a good 40 miles from home. She was getting ready to leave one day, Roberto and I decided to go with her and make a few bucks picking fruit. The old lady had a boyfriend that looked young enough to be her son. When we arrived at the fields, it was late in the day; and we became dumb and dumber not thinking about bringing a bedroll with us; his grandma lent us some blankets and we slept on the ground. Next morning about five thirty the pickers were ready to go pick fruit; we were not quite ready to go pick. After the pickers left, his grandmother was getting the meat ready to cook a stew for the workers; we stood watching her preparing the meat; the meat was loaded with maggots; she started scrapping the maggots off the meat and getting ready to cook. Roberto looked up at me shaking his head; we stepped to the side and decided this was not for us, time to go home. We did not even say our goodbyes. Not having wheels, the only way to get home was to thumb a ride. We left around six-thirty that morning, we walked some three miles before we reached highway 40. We walked and walked, no one would give us a lift. We spent some seven hours on the road with no luck; late that afternoon we reached a very long walk uphill; it took a good country mile to reach the top. The way up that hill was so dissolute no matter where you looked. We were about halfway up the hill, when I looked to the right side of the hill and all I saw was a jackrabbit running in the distance, and to this day I still call that hill, "Jack Rabbit Hill,". Every time I pass that area, it reminds me of that dreadful day; I even have my family calling it Jack Rabbit Hill. (That hilltop is now a big rig overnight stop). We reached the top and we could see the town of Vallejo in the distance; it was much different back then, than it is today. We make it to Tennessee St.; a good half mile down still no luck thumbing a ride. We were wondering how we were going to get across the bridge for we had money to take the bus across. Back then there was not much traffic to speak of. We reached Georgia St. Now! You will not believe what I am about to tell you!

Roberto's grandmother's boyfriend had come back to Richmond to pick some more supplies to take back to Roberto's grandmother; luck was with us when he saw us on his way back to the picker's camp. Back then highway 40 was only a four-lane highway; he saw us he recognized us; he made a U-turn to where we were walking, wondering how we got there. We told him the story. He gave us five bucks to take the gray hound bus, he drove us the bus station there in town. On to the Richmond gray hound station on 23rd. St. then from there another a long walk to first and Ohio Street. We got home about 6:00 P M. After a short rest we decided to go to the movies. We were in the theater a half hour or so, when my legs were in serious pain, and so were his; we had to come home, it was leg stress. A short time had passed, father did not like living there, so we had to move again. My parents knew a friend who lived in a private home on 5811 Jefferson Ave; just across highway 40 about four blocks from where the war apartments were where we once lived; the man decided to rent a portion of his house, it was the garage that he had converted to a living quarter, where his son lived. His son had moved out and it was vacant. The place had a front room, kitchen, and two bedrooms and a bath. Half block was Anglo's market on San Pablo Ave. and closer to El Cerrito high school. Another adventurous moment that happened at that house. One night, about One thirty in the morning, a big bang came from the front door that woke us up, someone broke into the house. My father, my mother and I were in bed with much fear; when two policemen with their pistols drawn and their flashlights shining on my parent's face walked up to them saying where is your son? By that time two other cops had come into my bedroom yelling, "Here he is." They jerk me abruptly out of my bed and place the handcuff on me. At that moment, another policeman from outside came in running and saying with a loud voice, "Stop, stop this is the wrong Joe Padilla they have captured the right one and is in custody." The flashlight went off and pistols were placed place back in holsters. The sergeant got on the radio talking with headquarters, he turned around and apologized to my folks with much embarrassment and told his men to release me, I was glad, for the cuffs were very tight on my wrists. The officer took time to tell us what had happened, saying, "It's amazing that two people with the same of Padilla and the first name of Joe and both of the same age of 18; born in February; when we received the report on a robbery on 23rd St. that was in progress and that the man had gotten away; and that he had a weapon on him, and was identified by the security cameras as a Joe Padilla, that was the only thing we were told, and the only name we found with that name was your son at this address. When I got on the radio a few moments ago, I was told that the Padilla we were looking for is from Rodeo not from South Richmond, once again, I apologize to you and the house owner," who was standing outside by the door; "The door will be fix." Early next day, the work on the door and wall was fixed. One Saturday afternoon, I went to the El Cerrito Theater, it was there that many of us kids would meet. I walked down the aisle looking for friends; I found one, it was a girl I knew from school, she had an unbelieved full breast I didn't know her very well as I sat there next to her we held hands and I slowly placed my arm around her and we kissed a few times I didn't mess around with her, I just sat there with her, when a lady came and got her and they walked out; I finished watching the movie thinking nothing of it. The following Monday, I was called to the principal office. I walked in and saw Mr. Palmer the school Principal surrounded by many people, and at the corner of the room was Shirley sitting there with tears in her eyes; yes, it was the girl I was sitting with at the El Cerrito Theater. I was being accused of getting aggressive with her in the theater. My heart started pumping extremely hard with fear. I was drilled and asked many questions unfamiliar to me as to where I had my hands placed on Shirley; I was asked again where I had placed my hands on her; I was in fear, as I replied, "I had my arm around her on her shoulder." It got silent for a moment. They looked at each other, then Mr. Palmer turned to Shirley and asked her where I had placed my hand, was it on her breast. He went on saying to her, "Remember, I want the truth." Talking about fear for I was a senior and she was a sophomore, she was maybe 16 and I was almost 19, and things did not look good for me. He asked her again as to where I had placed my hand; she was crying with fear. She looked up at her mother then at her aunt and uncle she replied sobbing as she slowly placed her hand on her right shoulder showing where I had my arm. She was asked again, and she replied with the same answer. Mr. Palmer asked me to step into another room, but the door was closed. I could hear them chattering but I could not make out what was being said. I sat wondering what I was going to tell my folks. After five or so minutes I was asked to come back in; everybody had left, only Mr. Palmer and I; as he spoke to me very calmly, "I'm sure you were telling the truth, but remember you are at the age where you have to be very careful when meeting girls; your record shows a very clean slate here at the school, and I noticed that you don't participate in any of the school activities, your teachers speak very highly about you and how artistic you are." I answered Mr. Palmer, "Sir, my parents do not have the money for me to participate in many school events where I can get back and forth and with that I just lay low." He said, "Son you are very lucky things came out good for you today, I will tell you what I will do for you. I want you to join the boy's club here at the school." After talking for a while, I agreed. This did change my life here at the school, I participated in many school events. Boxing was one of the things I mastered with the Boy's Club. One day we (the Boys Club) were invited to put on a boxing exhibition event at a club called, THE IT CLUB at the end of Potrero Ave. and San Pablo Ave. in El Cerrito, it was a very nice club, not your local beer bar, many high-class entertainers preformed there. That evening at the club we entered through the side door to a room because we were underage; from that room, one could see the floor show on the main stage. In the front of the band stood a beautiful young lady singing, she was well built, and had a beautiful voice, a real heartbreaker; everything was going along fine; when a sailor walked in the front entrance; the beautiful lady being an entertainer took a look as she was performing her song; she saw the sailor and she walked up too welcomed him, she then took hold of his hand and walked him to the stage, the crowd was cheering very loud and he was all smiles; when she finishes singing, she placed her arms around his waist and gave the sailor a big kiss, everyone stood up clapping and whistle. The beautiful lady left one arm around him and with her other arm she removed the wig from her head then she removed the false boobies from her chest, the beautiful lady happened to be a guy; that poor sailor turned bright red as he walked off the stage so fast and out the door.

The Last Padilla Standing

The house exploded with laughter. The entertainer was a female impersonator from San Francisco's Fein-oak-yo' Club known for its impersonator's performers. After a short break it was our turn. We went on with our boxing show. There were 8 of us paired off to box a three-round event. Yes, I won my boxing event that night. After that, I went on with my education. One sunny day, me and my school friends were having lunch at a local sandwich shop called the Gaucho just a couple of blocks from El Cerrito high school; that day I had on a brand-new sports jacket on, it was gray and purple and the gang were going on how great it looked except for one fellow, who was named Eddy (Ed) Garza he was one huge fellow who was about six foot and weight about 200 hundred lbs. I only weighed about 128 lbs and 5 foot 4 inches. We were all getting ready to go back to class when Ed started getting smart mouth over my jacket; he had a coke in his hand and started shaking it with his finger, as he removed his finger, his pointer at my new jacket and, of course, I had to say something. He replied, "What the hell are you going to do about it," and he started towards me and punched me. We got into it, he gave me two black eyes and I got him a couple of times that did not seem to bother him; when I went back to class, I was told to report to the office. I was asked by Mr. Palmer about with whom I had gotten into a fight with. I replied that I had bumped myself on a tree branch running between the buildings taking a shortcut. He knew better but I did not say anymore. Some years later, my wife, my daughter Ellen and I were at the San Francisco Zoo, and we bumped into Ed and his wife. We talked about old times, and he brought up about that day at the school and he apologized and told me that I had hit him on his left ear and that his ear still bothered him, no more was said as we went on. Back to my school days, the following year, I was 19 and doing well; when I was told to report to Mr. Homer who was the Dean of boys, wondering why I was called to the office. I entered the office and the secretary told me to take a sit that Mr. Homer would be with me shortly. It was not a long wait. He summoned me to come in and to take a seat. I sat wondering if I had done something wrong, that brought back the memories with Mr. Palmer and Shirley sometime back. What I am going to tell now, you will think it only happens in a movie or a story book, but this story is as true as I am sitting here writing my memories of that day. Mr. Homer looked at me and said, "Joe, take a seat." He paused momentarily before he spoke, I was wondering what I could have done wrong? He sat on the edge of desk and said, "The reason I called you, I was checking the boy's list because that's my job here at the school, as I was looking at your school record," he posed momentarily then said, "I had a different opinion of you, and I have an apology to make to you, after you had that meeting with Mr. Palmer sometime back, I judged you as a typical ruffian, so I decided to looked up your records and I went and talked with all the teachers that knew you; they all spoke highly about you, and that made me feel like a fool; for that I apologize that I wrongly judged you; I went and met your parents they told me you had gone with your grandmother, we had a long talk about your graduation which is coming up soon, I saw the poverty they were in and how they were worried about your graduation that you may not be able to attend; I took that into consideration; I have something to give you with an apology; you and I are the about same size and I have a suit that is a bit tight and I think it will fit you very well, please accept it with my apology." I was left breathless as he convinced me that it was alright. The suit was blue in color. I pick up the suit after school wondering what I will say to my parents! Maybe about Shirley and the past, not knowing if Mr. Homer had brought up that event. Everything went well. I am now a twelve grader and have a very good friend who lived near where I live; we became good friends, he hailed from Texas, and was called Tax; his true name was Bob Mumford, he lived with his mother as for his father, he was a war hero who died in the World War Two. One day we were talking, and he told a few things in secret about him and his girlfriend, he took a small box out of his coat pocket that he did not want his mother to know about; he went on telling me that, "every time she washes my clothes, she removes all my stuff out of my pockets, and I do not want her to find this. It was a box of 6 Trojans minus one (yes rubbers)." I was not acquainted with these things, I heard about them but never enter my mind; it wasn't like today; today, a kid of 13 who watches TV knows more about those things than I did when I was 18, Yes I was a virgin, I was not a party guy, my weekends were playing music in the honkytonks, and yes there was much going around in the bars, but I never play in the wild beer bars, I always played in older people clubs who were into dancing and having a good old time. This may sound somewhat strange in today's world, but I was brought up with respectable parents who taught me the facts of life and how to respect women. That does not mean temptation never entered my mind, I played around with girls, let us leave it at that. Now back to the trojans, I took them, and I put them in my jacket pocket not thinking anything about it, I got home hung my jacket in my room; it was late afternoon when my father called, he took me outside, said that he had something to talk with me about. He looked at me and said, "I was looking for some change and I saw your jacket and I looked and found this," holding the pack off rubbers. Uh-Oh, the time has come to have that father and son talk. He went on saying, "I just do not want your mother to find those things." With some embarrassment I explained to my father why I had them, he did not question me very much, he accepted what I had told him. We went back in the house and called Tax to come over immediately, I told him about what my father had found in my jacket pocket; I know my father was listening, as I was telling Tax to come and pick them up. When he arrived, he did not say anything. Tax came over as if nothing had happened, he just looked up at my father and smiled and we walked outside, and I handed him the box back and had a good laugh. I know father was peaking and laughing quietly. So went the day.

Chapter 10
Her Name Was Alta

The man who owned the house where we were living on Jefferson Ave. told my father that his son and his family were coming back home for his job was being eliminated within three months. This gave my father time to look for another house to rent and it did not take long. One block over on a street called Madison Ave. about a quarter of a block from the main Avenue, called San Pablo Ave. dad found a house for rent, so here we go again; we moved in. I had my own room; we were comfortable there. One Sunday, my sister came over to visit, she was about eight months pregnant, and she invited me to go to church with her; the church was about one block away on San Pablo Ave. it was called, St. John the Baptist. After the service was over, we walked out and were on our way home; standing at the front steps were a few women talking, when one of the ladies noticed that my sister was pregnant and she turned to the other women saying, "Oh look at this young couple;" All the ladies turned to look at us, as the lady continued saying, "So beautiful, and it looks like her time is coming soon." They were all chattering and smiling. We walked across the avenue and busted out laughing, what a story we had to tell mama, papa, and my sister's husband, Adrian. I was in the eleventh grade and going into the twelfth that coming year. That year I got a summer job at the Standard Realtor Co. in North Richmond, where my cousin Lupe worked; he picked me up every day, till, one day I was told to go on the swing shift the following week; I did not have a car and the last bus stop running at 10 pm. I met a friend there about my age who was also told to go on swing; he told me that he would pick me up. One night at work he told me that he had a 1932-dodge coupe for sale that ran very well and if I wanted, he would let me have it for $25.00, I agreed. He had a friend to take him home that night. OK! I now have my first car and a pink slip, the only trouble was that I had no driver's license and how to get home. The only driving experience I had was the driving school at El Cerrito Hugh School. It was a little after 1 am. I got in and started the car, I put it in gear it was different than the 1950 Chevrolet at school; it jerked some, but I was in control and on the road, I went with some fear for I did not have a license; I drove from North Richmond to home; I went through every back-street unknown to me. A week or so went by as I sneaked my way to work every night, I got used to driving the car and I studied the road manual; I was ready to get my license. The motor-vehicle dept. was on 22nd street. It did not take long. My turn came up; the instructor and I got in the car; he had a tablet and a pencil and said, "Let's go." I was told to drive to 23rd street. And turn left on Barrett Ave. then on to downtown Richmond. It was a cloudy day and it started to rain, when the instructor said, "We are not allowed to continue with this test due to the rain, but,seeing that you had driving training I will accept and continue on with your test; now, drive back to the Motor-vehicle department." We arrived and the driving instructor looked at me and said, "You passed." Oh yes: I passed my test, and even in the rain; everything went well. I did not have to sneak to go to work any longer, I would go on my own with a smile on my face. School started and I went back to school I felt good I had a car and many girls in the rumble seat. A short time had passed, and I sold my old 32 Dodge. As time passed, life was back to normal. One day, I went to the matinee at the Vista Theater, after the show was over, I bumped into a friend of mine, named Betty Napier, her brother was named Bill. Bill and I were good friends. Betty was standing there with the most beautiful girl I had ever seen. Betty introduced her to me; her name was Alta May Adams. as we stood talking, Alta noticed I had a St. Christopher metal around my neck, she reached over and looked it over; it was a metal my mother had given me; the metal had a blue glaze over it, it was unique and very attractive; she asked me if she could borrow it for a while. I was wowed over her then without thought, I took it off and handed it to her. A week went by, and I got worried about my St. Christopher metal; I did not even know where she lived; the only thing left for me to do was to ask Betty to show me where she lived. This was something I was hoping for, for she took my heart at first sight. She lived about five blocks away on Carlos Avenue from where I lived. I was well acquainted with that area; just across from the apartment where she lived was the Great East Shore Park where many baseball competitions were played. On the east side of the park was the grade school called, Stege where I went to the sixth grade, it was at that school on the way home that I experienced my first earthquake. School had just let out, I was on my way home, just across the street from the school was the North end of the East Shore park that had a fence that ran all the way along the sidewalk, the fence had a four inch board along the top; I decided to walk the on top board of the fence, I had walked a short distance when the earth started shaking, I was forced to jump off, it shook like forever, well, about twenty seconds give or take; I ran home a little frighten. I found out that it was a 4.3 quake. Now going on with the story about Alta; I was familiar with that area from the past, Betty and I reached the apartment, Betty knocked on the door, Alta opened the door and the first thing I saw was my St. Christopher metal around her neck. We talked for a while Betty told us that she had to go babysit. She left and we sat on the steps that went to the stairwell to the upper apartments. Alta handed me back my metal and asked me how I came about it; I told her that my mother gave it to me. We talked for a long while, it got dark, and I wondered why her mother had not come to check on her! So, I asked her where her father and mother were, for no one had come to check on her. She told me that her mother was working nights at a liquor store in Berkley, and her father was probably in a bar somewhere. I could feel the loneliness in her voice; I stayed with her until about 10 o'clock that night, I asked her if I could come and see her again. She replied by saying. "Of course, I will be here." "Maybe I can come over tomorrow?" I asked her; she reached for my hand and said, "I will be here, waiting." "What time?" I replied. She said, "Mama leaves about 3 PM and my dad has a drinking problem and he has gone around six till who knows when." I wanted to kiss her but, I did not want to be too aggressive and lose her friendship. In time we became awfully close you can say boyfriend and girlfriend we spent many hours in that stairwell talking. Why she picked me I am still in wonderment. She was so beautiful she could have picked any of the many boys who would go gaga over her. Many guys would look at her, then they would look over at me and they would look away as if not to get me agitated. One day we were going to the El Cerrito theater, we were getting on the bus, I was a bit slow checking my change for the fare, Alta was ahead of me and sitting nearby were two sailors when one started to flirt with her very strong; I walked up behind her and I looked at him, when he saw me, he looked and apologized, I must have had a stern look in my face. The next memories coming up are hard but true. As I mentioned before we sat in the stairwell talking for hours. She started to tell me about her parents; they were very good-looking folks, but do not let good looks deceive you. Her father's name was Hershel Adams; her mother's name was Dovie Adams; they hailed from Arkansas. Herschel was a bit prejudiced with me and her mother was the opposite and exceedingly kind. Alta told me that her father would come from work clean up eat and get ready to go bar hopping; he had a bad drinking problem. Her mother would take the bus around 3 in the afternoon to her work in Berkeley, working at the liquor store. Alta was left alone at night. We became awfully close we would kiss and hug but that was as far as we went. Remembering, that when you really love someone, respect is the number one rule that was the way I was raised. After meeting her parents, her mother learned to trust me and I was welcomed, she knew that Alta and I were meeting in the stairwell, so she approved of me coming into the apartment. She felt trust in me; we would sit and watch TV and do our homework; I would stay there till her father came home in the middle of the night, as for Dovie, she worked till two in the morning and would get home around three in the morning maybe later. As for my parents, I would call them and tell them that I was staying with my friend Jack; they trusted me; I was 19 and they did not know about Alta and me. I feel somewhat sorrowful talking about her parents, but this was my best friend. Life was so sorrowful for such a beautiful girl as Alta. She was loved very much by her parents and not knowing the damage they were doing to her mentally. She had so many beautiful things that any girl would cherish, but those beautiful things were only false and deceiving and very destructive. Many folks love the wild side of life and forget the life they created that is sitting alone at home in sorrow; two wrongs do not make a right. I feel blessed that I was there with her all those many hours as her parents were going downhill. Her father Herschel became an alcoholic and staying away from home; Dovie began gaining much weight, it was unbelievable. After a year or so, Dovie and Herschel were into too different worlds! Dovie became sinful and shameful in Alta's life. It is hard to talk about this but! I know that many out there have gone through similar event. Strange as it seems, I became Alta's caregiver. She was a very lonely girl, lost in a world of woe; I am grateful that I was there by her side. One event I witnessed, something that became somewhat shameful to Alta. (This, only Alta and I knew until now). That evening Alta and I were watching TV. Her mother was in her bedroom resting when a car started blowing the horn, and it went on and on without stopping; suddenly, her mother came out of her bedroom in such a hurry and all she had on was half slip and her panty, she placed her half slip over her breasts as she ran past us and out the door. We looked at each other wondering what this was all about. We went to the window to see; her mother was in a car with a man. She came back shortly and changed her clothes and told us she was going out with Bill. I know Alta felt embarrassed as she looked up at me, but she had trust in me knowing would not say anything to anyone. The next day we went to school, Alta was going to Portola High School about four blocks from The El Cerrito high school where I went; she was in the ninth grade, and I was in the twelfth grade. That afternoon I was called to the office that I had a phone call I thought maybe something had happened at home, I hurried to the office, the secretary handed the phone to me and walked away. When I said hello, it was Alta, she had gone home with reasons unknown. She was crying and sobbing profusely and that concerned me for she told me she was at home alone, and this left me wondering why she was in such panic! She then told me she was ready to end it all. (This part is rather difficult for me, for she was ready to end her life); I told her to wait till I got there, I ran out without telling anyone at the school that I was leaving. It was the distance of about two miles for me to get to her home. I ran most of the way; when I reached the apartment, I was lucky the front door was unlocked. I ran in looking for her, she was not in the front room and the room was filled with the smell of gas for she had turned the gas on the stove. This got me worried as I ran towards the bedrooms and onto the aisle-way, and I saw her sitting on the toilet, she was crying; as I approached her, I reached and opened the window and then ran back and shut off the gas. I returned to her and asked her what had happened. She turned looking at me sobbing and short of breath, as she reached for my hand and said, "my parents got into a furious argument and fight; father found out about Bill; he went out the door and mother returned to the bedroom and put her street clothes out and went out, maybe to work, I do not know." At that time, I did not want to ask her as to why she had gone as far as she had, so I comforted her and got her to settle down. We sat and talked about the many things that had gone so wrong with her parents. Sad to say, but! I was the only one she could lean on for she had no one or family to turn to. That evening we sat on the daybed, she had tears in her eyes as we talked. My mind was filled with sorrow and wonderment when a thought came to me! I thought it over and I talked with her about running away and get married; with tear field eyes she took hold of my hand and she agreed. *What to do, what to do,* entered my mind. The only place to get married would have to be Reno Nevada! She was 16 and I was 20 and we were still going to school; I had about two weeks before my graduation and knowing that my parents did not have the money for my graduation that was to take place at The Claremont Hotel in Berkeley California; so, I decided to drop out. So, done. We sat on the daybed thinking about how we could come up with an idea without her parents knowing what we had in mind. The next day was the weekend and her mother had stayed out all night with Bill, as for Hershel who knows???

Chapter 11
A Time to Elope

Now the time has come for me to figure out how we can get to Reno, Nevada. Being of a brilliant mind, a thought came to me as I talked it over with Alta. I told her I had found a way to get to Reno; she looked incredibly happy as she looked up at me and said, "What!" I looked up at her and said, "Do you think you could talk with your father if he would like to go with us to Reno for the day? She said, "I do not know if he would approve." I told Alta maybe she could sweet talk him into going with us; (my favorite two words) so done. Came Saturday morning, on May 20th, 1952, up and early the plan was working; I put on my blue suit and Alta had a beautiful blue dress: (I still have my suit, my tie and Alta's dress, still in incredibly good shape.) I knew that I had to have a little money, so I saved 60.00 dollars for this journey. The gas in the tank in my 52 Buick was full; we were on our way. Crossing the Antioch, Vallejo Bridge, back then, was only fifty cents to cross. Midway onto Sacramento, on highway 40 (now called, I- 80); passed Vacaville Ca. was, and still is what is called The Nut Tree. Back then it was a simple car stop, it had a genuinely nice restaurant and bar. We stopped to have breakfast; Herschel had a couple of drinks. Now, back on the road to Reno, straight ahead nearing the city limits I saw a bar up a way; when a thought came to me, as I whispered to Alta where Herschel could not hear me, "Do you think we can leave your father here at the bar while we go looking for a place where we can get married?" She whispered, "That, that was a good idea." That was easy. We told him that we would be back soon that we wanted to see the town, we left him there and we went on. When we approached the entrance to the city, there up high above our heads was a Hugh sign that read Welcome to Reno, The Biggest Little City: in the World. Reno was not like it is today everything was within walking distance; it did not take long to find a Justice of the Peace. We found a small place; as we entered, we were welcomed by a man that I believed to be a Judge or a Pastor, and a lady, who was his wife. We introduced ourselves and told them that we wanted to get married. They asked a few questions and asked how old we were; I told them I was 21 and Alta was 18; (that was a little white lie). The only thing he told us was the cost would be 23.00 dollars for the Marriage license, I paid up and they asked if we had a witness with us, I said no, he then said that it was OK that he had a fellow servant that would do us the honor and be our witness. WOW! That was quick and easy; we were man and wife within the half hour. It was customary to leave a tip for the services, there was a plate with money and envelopes on the way out; I did not have much money, so I handed them an envelope with 6.00 dollars, knowing that was way less than what was to be expected. We were so happy. Now back to where we left my new father-in-law. We arrived at the bar; outside of the bar was Herschel, he told us he thought that maybe we had forgotten about him and was worried, he had tears in his eyes. We picked him and we were on our way home as, man and wife. On the way we decided to stop at the Lake Tahoe Resort; and decided to rent a rowboat, so done. Hershel, now my father-in-law told us he would stay there at the club bar. We took off, it was great; I rowed down about half a mile and turned around to come back. When we left the boat Harbor the lake was so nice and calm, now, all of a sudden the wind came up, it was getting harder and harder to row, I would row one forward and the current would take us back three; it was tough fighting the current. We were out for some two hours, and I was not making any progress with my rowing. We were the only ones around, no one to help, when suddenly, we heard a motorboat coming towards us, it was Hershel who had rented a boat and a guide and went out looking for us, we yelled and all he did was wave back and they turned the boat back to port. It took another half hour to reach port; I was pissed but! What could I say? It was getting late and once more we were back on the road. We reached home about eleven: O'clock that night, we walked in and Dovie got overly excited wondering where we were all day; she got a little out of hand with Hershel. After things settled down, I left for home with a secret unknown to them that we were married. When I got home, I told my father and mother that we got married in Reno. Mama was jumping with joy and papa shook my hand and embraced me. How happy they were for me and Alta. They did not know Alta other than that she was my girlfriend. I told them that we had not told her father and mother about us being married just yet. I told them somewhat about what was going on between Dovie and Hershel. They did not question me, only to be sure to let them know. It was hard for me to wonder how to approach them. Two weeks went by, and we decided it was time to tell her parents. Alta and I talked it over That night while watching Melton Barilla on TV, I decided to speak up; I got their attention it was time to tell them the truth. I opened by saying, "I have something to tell both of you," I paused momentarily and said, "Alta and I got Married when went to Reno. " I thought I was going to get killed when Dovie turned to Herschel and yelled at him saying; "You Son of a Bitch! You let these young kids talk you into taking them," she couldn't say any more; with tear filled eyes she settled down. She came over to Alta and I and sat down looking at us. She looked up at me and said, sobbing, "I felt something like this was coming up, but not this soon." She paused for a moment and said, "Now! I want you to be sure to take care of my little baby." She started crying and reached over to us and put her arms around me and Alta, with tear-filled eyes I felt uneasy, as for Herschel, he said not a word. I remember saying something like this to Dovie. "We have not become united as husband and wife, not until we have your approval and a place of our own." I felt foolish saying this, but we were scared, what if our marriage would be annulled, I did not want Alta to be left stained, we had to restrain our desires. I went home that night. The following day, I took Alta to meet my parents; she was so welcomed, and my mother was so joyful and saying how beautiful Alta was. We stayed with Alta's parents for a couple of weeks. The first night we spent together was great and laughable not knowing what it was like to unite as husband and wife. A short time later, Hershel and Dovie separated, and we stayed with Dovie for a couple of weeks. I got a job as a machinist; I had to wait another week for my first payday. We decided to get an apartment of our own; it was a very nice apartment; it was a one-bedroom on a street called Ohio Avenue near Carlson Avenue. A month later I was laid off and with no money coming in, and Dovie had given up the apartment and she moved to LA with Bill. So, we moved in with my father and mother.

Chapter 12
That Little House on the Prairie

We had been married for about 3 months when we decided to have a child. My wife conceived we were so happy. At that time, the Korean War was hot, and I got my draft notices, that I was to go to San Francisco to verify my notification. Luckily, because my wife was pregnant, I was deferred. She was about three months along and doing well. One day, I had to go to my sister's place, I do not remember what for; she lived on State Avenue, about twelve blocks from where we lived. On my way back, I bumped with up an old girlfriend from school, we talked for a while, she started to get a little too friendly; I had to stop for things were getting somewhat out of hand as she started to take hold of my hand, and I felt bad for I had spent a little too much time BS-ing with her, so I yelled back and walked away thinking about my wife Alta for that morning she had what was thought to be morning sickness and that worried me somewhat. When I reached home, my parents were in the front room with Alta, she was crying, my parents did not know what was happening to her and did not know what to do. We took her back to our room and sat her down on a chair; my parents left us alone. (This is an unfavorable memory for me not knowing where to start). She stood up in her weakening condition and held in her hand what was the remains of what was to be our child, she had a miscarriage. I still remember that moment deep in my heart. Mother and I were attending to Alta and my father was calling emergency;

back then, we did not have ambulance services as we do today, so father called Doctor Benedict who was our family doctor; he told us to take her to the Doctor's Hospital on the 23rd street as soon as possible. Mother placed a blanket around Alta; Alta still holding her miscarriage on her hands. Back then, traffic was light not like today; I got to the hospital very quick and onto the emergency entrances in the back of the hospital. She was taken to the second floor, I followed them as far as I could, and I was told to wait outside the room. It only took about one-half hour when the doctor called me in and said that she was doing alright and that she would be weak for a couple of days. She was very weak, mostly from crying, and her body had not recovered from the shock that she had gone through, it took a while, but things turned out well for us. As time went on, I was in luck for I was called back to work. A couple of weeks went by, and we decided to move on our own again. We found a small place just across the East Shore Park on 5804-D on Cypress Avenue. The homeowner had two other houses in the back, ours was the third one at the end; it was more like a chicken shack, it was a wreck on the outside, but the inside was exceptionally clean. We called it, "The Little House in the Prairie." My parents also decided to move to a smaller place, and they found a place near to us on 49th. And Cypress Avenue. Once again, the military draft department sent me another draft notification they must have found out about my wife's miscarriage for I was inducted to duty on June 16, 1953, when the Korean War was at its highest and extremist conflict. My wife was left alone for 19 months in that little house in the prairie. Before my departure, my mother and my mother-in-law got together with us, and it was decided that we should get remarried in the church; the only church we knew was St. John the Baptist church on San Pablo Ave. We all want to have a talk with Father Flanagan who was in charge; he agreed to marry us that same day knowing that I am going to be deployed to duty that week. Now we were married by the law and by the church. Two days later I reported to duty, and was transferred to Fort Ord California. I was there for three days; this was where we received our mandatory medical shots. On the second day there, it was time for me to go get my shots; when I was in line the man in front of me told me that he did not like taking shots that he would pass out every time; as the line moved on it was his turn to receive his shot, sure enough down he went; when they came to pick him up I told the medic what he had told me about his passing out every time he got a shot; the medic told me that many men did that. It was my turn coming up, one medic on the right side and one on left, they grabbed my arms as they poked the needles into my arms, they left the needles hanging, when one medic said to the other. "Oh no, he flinched," he turned to me and said, "we have to give you the shots again;" they were giggling I thought nothing of it, yes, it was a prank, but being a greenhorn! Oh well, Life goes on. Those shots were triple typhus and triple tetanus. By nightfall I was one sick boy, I was very sore and every joint in my body was aching I was told it was a reaction to the typhus and the tetanus shots. Right then I realized why the two medics were giggling. I spend two days in my bunk. By then everyone had left for their assigned destinations; three days later I was the only one left, my turn came up and I was transferred to Camp Roberts to Company A of the 95th Heavy Tank Battalion. Camp Roberts was near Paso Robles here in California; upon arrival,

I was the only one dropped off from the military bus. I was all alone not knowing which way to go. Camp Roberts was a huge camp, and I was some five hundred miles from home, with no one to help me; but I managed. When there, I did not go through the usual eight weeks of basic training, mine were sixteen weeks of special training for I was placed with a Special Forces team, somewhat like the Rangers with the expectation of parachuting out of an airplane. I learned to fire many weapons more than the regular basic training guys. From light weapons to heavy weapons; from the 22 specials, the 38 calibers, and the 45 pistols, to the 30-06, M-1 rifle, the 30-caliber carbine, the water cool machine gun, the air cool machine guns, and the 50 caliber machine gun, the 80 light Mortar, to the 4.2 Heavy Mortar, and the 105 howitzers. The only tanks we saw were the ones that would run over our fox holes when we were in training. We learned how to use and clean all weapons, including two weeks of special hand-to-hand combat training. I graduated from my training on the last day of August 1953, waiting for the day of our departure, Korean bound.

The great day came; the captain and his cattery men were giving us our new orders, when he said, loudly, "There will be nine of you lucky bastards," he posed momentarily and repeated, "Nine of you lucky bastards will be going to Germany." He started calling out names, when he came to number seven, he yelled out "Padilla, Joe N." tears came to my eyes, for my prayers were answered, "no Korea"; two more were called out, one was a new friend called Ed Macmillan he was from Richmond also. The rest of the troops were sent to Korea. The first thing I did was to call Alta, and my parents with the good news. When we graduated, we were given a week's leave before our deployment to New Jersey. The following week, we took a flight from San Francisco to Camp Dix in New Jersey, and from there on to Bremerhaven Germany on the USS Gen. Alexander M. Patch; a troupe Ship with 1500 hundred tropes aboard. Pre-boarding, We were told that we were not allowed to bring any instruments aboard, it so happened that I had my double-neck Fender steel guitar with me, I had to find a way to take it with me or lose it; all I had was my duffel bag and a short time to come up with something; the only thing for me to do was to give away half of my clothing and make room for it in my duffel bag for my steel guitar; so, done. This only made my duffel bag somewhat heavier. On our way out from the harbor limits, the P A blasted out 'NOW HEAR THIS - NOW HEAR THIS, - IF ANY OF YOU LUCKY BASTARDS HAPPENED TO HAVE SNUCK YOUR GUITARS OR UKE'S REPORT TO THE SPECIAL SERVICES OFFICER ON DECK. Uh, oh, there goes my guitar was my thoughts. When I reported on deck! Everyone seemed to be incredibly happy, there were about six men holding their instruments in hand; when the Lieutenant asked me where was my instrument and what it was. I said, "It is my steel guitar, Sir, it is in my duffel bag." The Second Lieutenant replied, "Go get it." When I returned, I had a fear of losing my steel. The Lieutenant then said, "Time to set up." I did not understand what he meant. He looked at me and said, "Well don't just stand there, set it up." I thought to myself! This is weird, I really did not know what was going on! The reason was! I came up somewhat late for I was in the third deck below and did not hear about the event that was coming up on the following night. When I saw the other fellows ready to play, I then told the Lieutenant, "Sir, I don't have an amp." He replied, "That's the last thing in mind, we have plenty; now we have a get it together for tomorrow we have a show to put on." *Wow! Is this for real?* were my thoughts. We became one great country band overnight. That consisted of, a country singer, who was the Lieutenant himself, A base player two guitar players a fiddle player, and yours truly on steel. We were on the upper deck that was off-limits to us enlistment men. The time came we went on stage and to our surprise there were so many women and officers. I found out later those women were GI wives going to unite with their GI husband overseas. One thing I witnessed was the behavior of the women, whose behavior was so disgraceful and without shame; I will leave it there. I became the star for the night; after the performance, the Lieutenant asked me if I would like to be the ship's radio and music announcer for a few hours a day. Oh, yes! Though I was somewhat seasick, I agreed, I played many requests, from the troops aboard, mostly country music. The ship had an array of different types of 78 and 45 music records. The following day a rumor came about that ranking three officers, and three of the ladies were cut romancing; and that the three officers were dishonorably discharged on the spot, as for the ladies they received papers of legal separation and possible divorcement they were returned, back to the U. S. A. they never left the ship; they returned home to face their imbursement. This, I was told in secret by the Lieutenant, mum was the word. As we were entering the English Channel we were in heavy fog, I was in my bunk when, the P A, blasted out, "NOW HEAR THIS NOW HEAR THIS IF YOU WANT TO SEE THE CLIFFS OF DOVER, YOU BETTER HURRY,

YOU HAVE ABOUT 15 MINUTES BEFORE THE FOG COVERS THEM UP AGAIN." The deck was covered with GIs; the announcer was right, the fog covered everything very quickly, we were lucky to have seen the Cliffs of Dover; we were told it was very rare at that time of the year. We arrived at The Bremerhaven Harbor in Germany at mid-day. What a welcome we had. Fifteen hundred troops lined up to be assigned to our permanent location. I have never seen so much brass in one spot. Now came the big build-up; how proud they were for us to be standing waiting for our permanent placement. A Major stood at the microphone as he pointed to a big red one surround in a green background. Just under the big red one was written, "No Mission too Difficult, no Sacrifice too Great, and Duty First." He continued, "There will be nine of you lucky bastards (sounds familiar?) to be assigned to the Big Red One." O yea, I was number seven once again, but that was not all; as he continued saying, "Two of you lucky dogs, will go with the 16th. Infantry. To the Home of the Rangers, may God have mercy on you" Lucky me, I was number one and my friend from Richmond, Ed Macmillan was number two. The other seven went to the 18th. And the 26th INF. We were placed on a train from Bremerhaven to Frankfurt, from there onto Schweinfurt home of the 16th. Inf. Rangers. When we reached headquarters, we were asked what kind of duty we had in mind! We just looked at the corporal, as he said, "We trying to place you with something you are familiar with." I replied, "I like working with radios". Ed said, "I like auto mechanic." The corporal gave us our destination. Ed was assigned there at that post to the motor pool; I was sent to the heavy Weapons garrison as a field radio operator; some three miles west. I was taken there by jeep.

Upon arrival, I walked into the office, and the corporal took me right to the captain's office I placed my duffel bag on the floor and saluted and introduced myself. "Sir, Joe N. Padilla reporting for duty, Sir" my duffel bag hit the floor somewhat hard, and this alarmed the captain; he asked, "Son, what do you have in that duffel bag?" I stood in attention and replied, "Sir, t is my steel guitar, Sir," He said, "At ease, at ease, son;" He paused temporarily then continued with a smile on his face saying, "You play the steel guitar?" "Yes Sir:" I replied. He continued by saying, "You got here just in time; we are having a company gathering at the EM Club (The Enlisted Men's Club.) this weekend in honor of Colonel Mott, the Commander in Chief of the 1st Infantry Division." He smiled and said, "You will be rooming with the third squad where the boys are putting a country band together, I'm sure you will be more than welcome." He called the corporal and said, "Take this man and introduce him to the third squad, he will be bunking there." As we arrived and the corporal introduced me to the third squad saying that I was going to bunk with them, and that I was a steel guitar player. Boy! What a welcome I had. There were three guitar players, one was a lead guitarist, two rhythm guitarists, a fiddle player, and a base player, and now yours truly on the steel guitar. We had two days to get ready. The gathering is to be held at the EM Club. The following night everything was ready as we set up for the coming event. Up front was the table set up for Colonel Mott and company. I was a bit worried playing with these guys for the first time but, they were very good as I stood playing alongside them; we had a great time, and ready to go.

Chapter 13
TDY — Permanent Temporary Duty

Opening night; some GI brought their wife, others brought their Fraulein (German girlfriends), and 80% GIs; we had a full house. On stage, Captain Hall told everyone to stand for the National Anthem; so, done. Colonel Mott was introduced by Captain Hall, everyone was standing at attention. Then told to be seated. The Colonel stood up and walked up to the mike and introduced himself. After his speech, He looked over to where his wife was sitting at the table to the left of the stage, he asked her to come forward so he could introduce her. (You will not believe this one)? As she got up and started walking across the floor, the place went momentarily silent, then! WOW! What a gorgeous lady dressed in a very tight light grey net dress walking across the floor. All one's eyes were upon her; Look out Betty Grable, look out Marilyn Monroe, this was the Goddess Venus. She looked to be about 38 give or take, she looked young enough to be the Colonel's daughter. After all the clapping and whistling it was time to start. I started the intro with the "roadside rag," from then on, I was the star of the night. After two hours of playing, it was time for a break. The jukebox was turned on; as I stepped down from the stage, I heard someone calling me, it was Colonel Mott, and he called me over to his table. My thoughts were maybe that he wanted a special request. I reached the table and saluted him, he said, "Stand ease son, stand ease, come take a seat," The Colonel looked up at Captain Hall, then said, "Hall, this man needs to be in special service." Captain Hall agreed. After the bragging was over, they were convinced that I was to go on to special service, and way down deep so was I. I stood up ready to leave, the Colonel stopped me once again and said, "Son! Will you do me the honor of dancing with my wife she loves to dance, and I don't know how, I have two left feet." I know I must have looked surprised as I answered, "It will my pleasure and my honor, Sir, I walked over to where she was sitting my eyes went in circles looking at her beauty; she smiled and stood up and took hold of my hand and walked with me to the floor. I could feel the GIs looking with envy. The jukebox started playing "Till I waltz again with you." She was very friendly and asked me how long I had been playing the steel, and how she loved the sound of the steel guitar, I answered the best I could being rather shy; we continued dancing. When we finished, I walked her to where she was sitting, the Colonel thanked me. I returned to the stage. On the second break, the Colonel called me back and asked me if I would dance with his wife once more. (What makes you think I would say no? Just do not, tell my wife.) When we returned, the Colonel told me to take a seat. He said, "Son I would like for you to join the Special Service, your rank may be frozen, but you will be compensated on the side; those GIs need entertainment, a lot of these boys have been away from home for a long time and are lonely for home memories to forget the misery of war, you can see that in here, now, I will leave that up to you," he thanked me. I said, "Sir, I will be delighted and honored, Sir," As I returned to put my guitar away, the guys wanted to know what magic I had and what it was like dancing with a goddess. Now I have a confession to make, I never told my wife about me dancing with the

Colonel's wife, I felt sorry for her sitting at home and thinking that I was having a good time without her. A short time had gone by, and I was called to the office. Captain Hall asked me why I never put in for a weekend pass. I told him I had no reason to go anyplace and that I enjoyed going to the EM club and enjoyed a drink or two and sitting in the library reading and writing to my wife. We talked for a while, and he ordered me to take a couple of days off and to go with the boys to a local Pub. That weekend I went out with the boys, they managed to get me tipsy; the next day, I woke up in my bed as I sat up and looked at floor and to my surprise next to my bed were two guitar amplifiers the boys had bought for me from the local people. Two weeks went by just waiting. One morning I got called to go to the office to pick up my Permanent TDY (permanent temporary duty) papers and that I was to go with the special service bus waiting for me outside. I placed my gear in the bus and was driven to Wurzburg Germany some 25 miles from Schweinfurt where the Special Service unit was stationed. I reported to a lady named Mrs. Hanson who was a civilian worker for the Armed Forces, she was the one in charge of all the special service group. After many months of entertainment, many of our boys in the group were discharged and we became a smaller unit; and after a couple months there, the only one left was yours truly. Ms. Hanson returned to the USA. I was the only one left with some forty empty beds except when the baseball or the basketball teams, or a road show would come to play there at the post, I was left in charge of the billet on the third floor. One day I was told that there was going to be a General Inspection and that the General of the post was going be the inspector; I was all alone taking care of the third floor with some forty empty beds minus one, yours truly, and I had only one day to get the place clean and make ready for inspection. We did not have lockers on that floor; each bed had a footlocker that sat at the front of every bed. In the front of my bed where my footlocker sat, is where I had all my personal belongings, and the windowsill was my nightstand; I also, had a cloth rack that I acquired from the man's room to hang and place my uniform and my other clothing. After making up all the beds to specification one by one, I was ready come what may. Next morning about eleven O'clock I heard the inspection team coming up the steps; I hurried to the front of the dormitory. They came in, I stood in attention as I responded. "Sir: the quarters are ready for inspection." The General and his staff walked around looking, when, they came up to my bedding, they stopped, and the General asked me who that equipment belonged to. I replied, "Sir: these are my assigned quarters, I am the overseer to all the special service visitors when they arrive, under the orders of Captain Peck, the special Service officer, Sir," The General turned and looked over at the base Captain; they were talking over my situation, at that moment I was afraid of being sent back to Schweinfurt, goodbye gravy train were my thoughts. When, the Captain turned to me and said to me, "Private, I was not aware of this; you will share quarters with the Mail Clerk downstairs." *Wow!* Were my thoughts, knowing that the mailroom was a very private and secluded room for the US Mail only, yet! I was trusted to room with the mail Clark. Just before they were ready to leave, I was told how well the inspection went, and to report tomorrow to the Captain Peck's office there in the garrison, and that he would have a talk with him. That day, I moved in with the mail clerk downstairs. The following morning about 8 AM, I arrived at the special service office. It was only a couple of buildings down facing the front street, and on to the second floor just above the Gym; this was where Captain Peck's office was. I walked in and introduced myself and I was welcomed by Captain Peck; he introduced me to his office personnel, there were three other persons there, a Sergeant named Joe Wilson, and two German ladies, one was his personal secretary named Elizabeth, the cute one, the other secretary was named Elsa an elder lady, who was sergeant Wilson's secretary, and she became my secretary also. There was one more person, a Sargent Muthaura, who was over the Gym activities downstairs he had his own office and was seldom seen. Captain Peck assigned me to the special service entertainment dept. I was given my own desk, my duties became, Edgerton Clerk, Administration Clerk, Entertainment Clerk, Stage Engineering, and Mail Clerk, all this came along with a Volkswagen Van. Written on the sides of the van was painted in big letters, Special Service US Army, all came along with a permanent overnight pass. What the hey, either that or go back to the Heavy Mortar Company: no way. As time went by, I escorted many live shows to many Army garrisons in West Germany. In all that time, I had only had one incident that happened on my watch. One day on the way to an EM Club, (Enlisted Man Club) at the Katzenstein Army Post. I booked a group that called themselves The Swing Your Partner show, they hailed from Canada. It was a square-dancing group; they had a four-piece band and nine girls that would go into the crowd and invite the soldiers to square dance with them, many guys did not know what square dancing was, the girls would pick different soldiers out of the crowd, it was so great to see the enjoyment on the GIs faces. When I first booked them, the name Georgia Brown came up, I thought it was a woman singer! Well, we only roomed men at the camp; I had to find a hotel room for her in downtown Wurzburg. When they arrived, Surprise, surprise, Georgia Brown was the band leader, not a woman; though they did have nine girls with them. I got on the phone, and I got a hold of the Women's Army Wax Section there at the base; I told them I was from the Special Services Dept. just across the field and asking if they could accompany the nine girls from a road show there in their billets who needed lodging: so, done. Now back to the incident, that I had scheduled at the Katzenstein army post some 20 miles away. We were on the road, I was sitting in the front seat just across the Bus Driver; I could hear some serious talk with one of the girls and the guy called Georgia, it went on for a while! When suddenly the emergency door at the back of the bus slammed open; the door alarm went off, and the girls started screaming and yelling to stop the bus. The bus driver could not speak English and I could not speak German, and the only word I knew was halt; the bus came to a stop; I ran to the back and saw one of the girls laying on the road, I jumped down to see; when I reached to where she lay, she looked to be in serious condition; thank God she was not dead. I asked the group if they knew what had happened no one said a word. When the one called Georgia Brown, came up to me to tell me what had happened. He said that he and the girl were having a love affair. He went on to tell me that his wife had just had a baby, and he told the girl about his wife having the baby and he had to break up their love friendship. It was obvious she could not take the lies he had told her, and short of living! She decided to open the exit door in the back of the bus jumped. I was not ready for all this, and I knew I had to make a report on this incident. Not knowing how to get in touch with my Captain, and unable to speak with the driver. Luck was me, a jeep with three army officers and a driver came from the opposite direction and saw me waving and they stopped. They asked me what had happened. I half-assed told them what I knew; they looked at the girl, she was badly injured but conscious. They picked her very carefully and placed her on the jeep; they managed to make a stretcher with what they had. The officer in charge told me he would report this to the MP. When the MP arrived, I had to make an incident report the best way I could. The MPs. Told me they would get a hold of me later. They turned and spoke in German with the bus driver unknown to me what was said. After that, the bus driver and I took the people back to Wurzburg. When we returned to camp, I went straight to the hospital to see how the Girl was doing. Georgia met with me there in the aisle way telling me what a nice girl she was and went on telling me that I should try to hook up with her. Boy, did he have the nerve. The following night the show went on and things went well after that, minus one girl. I was not informed as to whatever happened to the Girl, I wished her well. As for Georgia?? After that incident, many more shows and many more happy GIs were entertained. I enjoyed seeing their happy faces.

Chapter 14
My Last Day of Duty

My time was coming up, and time to go back to my unit in Schweinfurt. I had a short time to go before I headed home. On my last day of field duty with the sixteen-infantry; the unit went on a field trip where we setup the 4.2 heavy mortar in a combat-ready placement; and seeing that I was the radio operator, a driver, and a short timer me and the other drivers were placed on road duty, that was so no one would enter the danger firing area. We were set about 4 miles apart from one another in the middle of nowhere and with no radio, it was just me and a four-foot billboard that stood up high on a 4x4 post setup with nothing but open land all around. The day was slowly passing by. Sometime after sunset as it was getting dark, I looked up, and about eight hundred yards in front of me, I saw a huge wild boar coming towards me following the dry creek bed. The only thing I had was my M1 and no ammo; I was lucky the wind was blowing my scent in the opposite direction away from the wild boar. I got behind the skinny 4x4 post on the billboard; yes, I was scared, that pig looked to be well over 500 lbs. As I stood watching all l I could hear was that pig grunting and my heart pounding furiously; thank God the pig followed the dry creek bed. With my heart pounding so hard, I just sat leaning against the post. The company commander had forgotten about me. I looked at my watch it was passed 9 PM. I had been on watch from around 10 O'clock that morning. I kept looking down the road when I saw car lights coming towards me hoping it was ours. It was a ¾ ton truck with the other guys that were left behind also; I was the last one to be picked up. We reached the camp at about 11 PM. we had not eaten all day and all we had that night was a skimpy lunch of baloney and bread. Two days later, Ed and I were picked up and taken to the Frankfurt Army Air Base. From there, my friend Ed and I were escorted and placed on an old B 17 bomber converted to a twelve-personal carrier. There were the two pilots, twelve men and two military airline hostesses in that airplane. We were well on our way over the ocean when the pilot made an announcement; that there was a small problem with the plane and that we were landing in Iceland for a quick fix. I could tell the airline hostesses were a bit on edge just looking at them. We arrived at the air base; our delay was about six hours. All that time we had not had anything to eat since we left Frankfurt. Left hungry we were told to board the plane and we were on our way once again. On the way, one of the airline hostesses was asked what the trouble was. She told us that the engines would not reverse, so they had to land on a longer airstrip for the plane to come to a full stop. When we left Iceland, the plane followed the Canadian coastline all the way to New Brunswick in the New Jersey airfield at a very high altitude, not the usual route, reason unknown, maybe precaution. Finally, someone spoke up that we had not eaten since we left Frankfurt. When we arrived at the airfield, it was after hours and the kitchen was close. We were taken to an open all-night cafe, where all we had was one Hamburg, and a hand full of French fries and coffee; we spent the night there at the army billets. The next day at 5 AM in the morning, we had a quick breakfast; by 6 AM we took a two-engine plane on to Chicago; there we had a couple of hours stop; that is where I ate and made a phone call home that I would be arriving at San Francisco sometime late that afternoon. From there we were placed on a TWA, and on to Denver. When we arrived at the Denver airport, a few passengers were picked up, it was a 45-minute wait, I made another telephone call home, that we had a delay in Denver and would arrive in San Francisco sometime late afternoon; it turned out somewhat better, the delay was a quick one. The plane landed about 11:45 that morning. On arrival, my cousin Lupe (now deceased) was there waiting for me, he had called the airport and found out that my flight would arrive at the S. F. Airport around twelve noon. Cousin Lupe saw me and what a welcome I had. We arrived home; he dropped me, my guitar, and my duffel bag at the front of the main house. It was about one o'clock in the afternoon. Cousin Lupe told me that I should go in and be alone with Alta before I go see the rest of the family, I agreed. I got out of the car and walked on to that 'little house in the prairie,' I stood at the front of the door, at that moment I did not know whether to knock or just open the door? So, I knocked on the door lightly, she replied, "Come on in Bea," Alta thought it was her best friend Bea, knowing that I would not be getting home until late that day. I opened the door slowly she was sitting on the daybed, propped up on two pillows listening to the radio. I suppose she was thinking about my arrival. She stood up and stood motionless in front of me, as we just stood there looking at each other like we were strangers. It was so hard for me to think right at that moment after nineteen months of separation; it felt like I had just met her; I was in a dreamworld just looking at such a beautiful young lady standing before me. We stood looking at each other not knowing whether to hug and kiss? With tear-filled eyes we embraced. The separation made that moment anew, with a new start in time lost. We sat on the daybed with tears in our eyes, we became comfortable holding each other trying to replace the moments of lost time passed. An hour had passed by, I took a shower and refreshed myself. Alta cooked a quick lunch for me; it was time for me to go see my parents and her parents and the rest of the family. Another moment of happiness and tears lay ahead.

Chapter 15
A Time to Adjust

We stayed there at what we called the little house in the prairie for some time. I had little money from my last army check, enough to buy an old 1936 Dodge Coup. That coup almost took my life one day; I was working changing the plugs when I placed my hand on the ignition coil, Woah Boy did get the shock of my life! it took my breath away and paralyzed my right arm, I had a tough time getting the circulation back to normal. Take my advice be careful where you put your hands when working on an old car. After I finished, we went for a ride and picked up her best friend Bea and her boyfriend who was called Tax, a tall lanky fellow very countryfied and very funny, so off we went reminiscing memories of a time gone by, and on to the old hang-out place just across the street from the Vista theater where we sat and made plans for the day; we had a real good time. That night Alta and I sat making plans and thinking what to do with our lives? I was home for about a week when I got a job as a machinist. The following day at work, a thought came to me, I had just received my mustered out pay from the military over $900.00 wondering what to do with that money was in my mind. We were having lunch when I heard one of the workers talking that he had just bought a house and I remembered how hard it was to rent a decent place. Living with the memories of our parents never having a home they could call their own, and with that in mind I spend the day in thought. That night Alta and I sat back

The Last Padilla Standing

talking things over about buying a house. We started looking through the newspaper. Back then, it was hard to qualify when buying a home; I was depending on my GI bill or my Cal-vet plan, and they were somewhat hard to get. The easiest way was to go through a VHF home loan. After looking, I could not qualify for a home in El Cerrito, we could not qualify for a home in the East Richmond Heights so back to the lower parts of town. Back then the town of San Pablo was just a subsidiary of Richmond not well known till it got its independence and became the city of San Pablo, no longer a subsidiary of Richmond and now, known as The Plaza De San Pablo. As you enter San Pablo Ave. and the end of 23rd St., is road 20 the beginning of the Al Portal Plaza, the home of New Berry's, Longs, Mechanics Bank, Gabardine's, and McDonalds; and in the backside of the plaza facing road 20 was where Simmons hardware, and the Marvin's clothing store that was located just off Road 20 that went across San Pablo Ave. and ended on Rumrill Blvd. Just across San Pablo Avenue was The Star Club, and down about three blocks or so was Casper's Hot Dogs, and on to Broadway Ave. That was and still is downtown San Pablo. Going south on San Pablo Ave. we approached Church Layne, where the St. Joseph Catholic Church has been a landmark for many years. We followed the road till it ended on 23rd. St. from there was the start of Market Ave. where we started looking for a house on both sides of Market Ave. that ended on 13 St. where we flip a U-turn back up Market Ave; we approached 16 St. Suddenly, my wife said, "Look there's a for sale sign on that little white house." We took the phone number went home and called the realtor. He came right over and took us to look in the inside of the house; "wow," said my wife; it had two nice-sized bedrooms and a large, detached garage. Price, $9,000,500, with that price we did qualify. We did all the paperwork and within less than a month, we were ready to move in. About three months later Alta was with child, and we decided to have my mother-in-law Dovie, to move in with us to help Alta. She stayed with us for quite some time. Ellen was born on December 16, 1955, about 4:00 P M. One day later Alta and Ellen were home. After some six-month Dovie moved out. Around 1957 jobs were hard to get and we had an extremely hard time, and we almost lost the house a couple times. I jump from job to job many times. We lived on my unemployment checks and credit at the local grocery store. As time moved on, my father-in-law Herschel, had a hard time and he moved in with us. I could still feel the resentment he had over me, maybe for marrying his daughter. One day, he went to the grocery store, when he returned, he was all smiles which was unusual, and very talkative. Later that afternoon I had to go get some groceries and picked up a few things we needed, when I came up to the store clerk, I told him to put it on tab. He looked at me and said, "Sorry you can't have any more credit here and you have to pay your bill within a week." Later in time, we found out from a good friend of our that was in the store when he heard my father-in-law talking to the store owner and that it was him who had my credit stopped there at the store. For a man to do something like this to his own daughter is unheard of. A short time later my father-in-law moved out, thank God. This left us with a hard time. Another thing came about! my wife's aunt and uncle had moved nearby; they hailed from Arkansas she was called Boots, and her husband was called Arval; one weird couple; Boots was a very loose woman and tried very hard to stain my wife in her dirty way of life, but Alta knew her very well and that ended that. They had a son named Micky, I felt sorry for him; he had a very hard life through his younger years. But he turns out to be a very nice person unlike his parents. They moved back to Arkansas in the mid 70s. his parents passed on, and a few years later Micky passed on also. One day I bumped into an old friend named Jack, who knew a guy that was supposed to be a great country singer and that he was looking for musicians to start a weekend country band. Jack begins telling me, that he had told the guy about me playing the steel guitar and that he wants to meet me. He was already playing with another fellow, at a place called, The Hide-Away, and they were looking for a third guy. That night I talked it over with my wife for this would bring a little money so needed; she agreed; so, I called my friend to bring him over to meet me and my wife. Next afternoon they arrived we introduced our self. The singer was named Arron Smith, better known as Smithy; he was a very handsome man, he was one of those people who would start talking and keep your interest listening to his conversation; a very friendly person. He brought along his wife, she and my wife befriended right away. Smithy told me that he heard that I was a good steel player and wanted to know if I would join them. I looked up at my wife she just sugared he shoulders. I told him that he has not heard me play. He said, "That is no problem, I have my guitar in the car." He returned and we set up. What a voice this man had, he did not need a mike he was loud and clear. Later we were talking; I asked him how he got started singing? The story of his mother came up and he told me that she had been an opera singer back in her heyday. Right then I realized where he got his strong singing voice. We played at a pub called The Hide-A Way on Carlson Blvd, near the Supply Armory center. Fifteen bucks a night, plus tips, and that two night a weekend did help. Smithy and I were talking at break time he then asked me where I was working at. I told him that I was not working and that I have had a hard time finding a job. He looked at me he then changed the subject and asked me if I was afraid of high. I did not know what to say and why he asked me such a question, he just looked at me and smiled as he continued saying, "I work for a glazing company in San Francisco that works with glass windows and panels on high-rise buildings, I was thinking if you don't mind working on a scaffold you got a job working for me." Wow was all I could say. He replied, I will pick you up tomorrow at 7 am. I worked with him for over two years. Things got slow he had to let me go. That same day, Smithy was talking with a man, and he called me over and intruded me to him; he was one of the Cobble-Dick, kibbe Glass Co. supervisor; after talking with me for a while he asked me if I did not mind driving a large truck to and from the job, he would give me the job. I worked there for a quite few months; work got slow again I got laid off. Once again, Smithy came to the rescue, he got me on with the Kawneer Store Front Co. on Parr Ave. in North Richmond where I worked for 13 years plus. It was there that a friend I work with had a daughter working as a sectary with BART (Bay Aira Rapped Transit) in San Francisco when it was first starting in 1968; he picked an application for me from his daughter. Three years had gone by, and it got forgotten. After 13 years, Kawneer closed and moved to Visalia California, but did not take anyone from Richmond with them. Once again, I found myself jumping from job to job. I was working for the International Harvester company in North Richmond. I had been working there for over a year when I received a phone call from The Bay Area Rapped Transit to come in for an interview at the Richmond BART yard on, 13th and Lincoln, with a Mr. Damco. Damco was looking for a specialist and he saw that I had worked as a mechanic and as a glazer; (that is, working with glass). Luck was with me he was looking for someone to work on the windows on the BART car', I was hired on the spot till I Retired in 1996 after 25 years. I would have stayed a couple of years longer but my wife was ill, and, on the wheelchair, I became her caretaker; she was going in and out from hospital to hospital and thank God I had a good health plan that carried on when I retired, it paid for all the many times going back and forth from hospital to hospital with my wife, and only the co-payment was all I had to pay. The only thing the insurance would not pay for, was for a caregiver and I could not afford one, I was with her all those years until she passed on, August 12, 2005. May she rest in peace.

Chapter 16
Stolen and Sorrow

There comes a time that becomes difficult to explain in detail on something not quite understandable without involving someone in the family, but what I witnessed is true. Now, as I go on with my biography. The last time I visited the Pueblo's in New Mexico where my mother's family lived, was sometime in the mid-1970s. My sister and my brother-in-law were getting ready to go visit his only remaining aunt Raina in a town called Pena Blanca New Mexico, a few miles from where my mother's family lived in a town called Sile. I had just started my two-week vacation. Adrian talked us into going with them; we followed them not knowing the way. When we arrived, we were introduced to his aunt Raina; she was a very unusual and talkative person; she talked a lot about witchcraft and other odd things to do with the local natives' spiritual ways and things I did not understand and did not care to know. We spend three days there. On the first day, it was decided to go visit my birthplace, Madrid. Early that morning we piled in my car and off we went; it was some 40 miles give or take. We arrived at Madrid from the Albuquerque side of the town; things began to familiarize in my mind. As we moved on to front street, just below the hillside was where the old power plant with the three huge smokestacks stood for many years welcomed me. To my surprise, the plant had become a museum with the history of Madrid's past. We parked and went to the entrance where we met an older man, who was the gatekeeper; I introduced myself and told him the story of my life here in Madrid pre-1940. After the introduction, I asked him if he may have known or heard of the Padilla family who had lived here for many years. He replied that he had only lived there for only a few years and was not familiar with anyone from the past. The entrance fee was $1.50 per-person, I was ready to pay for all of us when he said, "No charge," that this was a welcome back to my place of birth. I thanked him. He decided to give us a tour of the museum. We were told to stay in a group. As we were walking, I noticed Raina and her friend had left the group and took off on their own knowing that the rules were, that we were supposed to stay together. As we entered the first site that struck me was the movie camera setup from the old movie house at the end of town; it had a row of seats; who knows I may have sat in one of those seats way back then. We walked on and he showed us so many things familiar to me, such as the batteries that were used with the headlamps the miners used back then to illuminate their way in the mines; I am sure my father and grandfather must have used one of them, for it was take one from the rack every day. We saw many picks and shovels that brought memories of the sweat and tears of time past if only they could tell the stories. After a lengthy time with the man, Raina and her friend quietly cut up with us and no one had paid any attention to their absence except me. It was time to leave, I thanked the man for his kindness and that we appreciated the tour; I gave him a nice tip. From there we went to the other side of town to where the base ballpark was. We arrived at the ballpark and not knowing it was private property we drove across the ballpark to the other side; when a pickup truck approached us; we were asked what we were doing there. After I explained to them my story and showed them the many houses where we once lived and just above the ball stadium where the traces of the old, converted garage used to sit; I then pointed across the arroyo to the house where we had lived before, we left for California in 1942 during the World War Two, the house was still standing. They welcomed us and told us to continue. We drove to the back of the baseball stadium on to the top of hill to where we once we lived; the only things that was left were the reminiscence of the old, converted garage where we once lived. Just a short way was the remnant of the old out-house. We looked around for a while; then drove to the top of the ridge and I remembered one of the old trails that went to where my grandmother's place once stood. It was down the steep hill and about a good half mile north. I was telling my kids how we used to go visit grandma's place and asked them if they would like to take a hike and see where the old ranch once stood; they got overly excited. I then asked Adrian if he would like to go with us; I could tell that he did not believe what I was telling him, for all he could see was wilderness and a steep hill; so, agreed. The four of us, Adrian, Tim, Liz, and I; started walking down the old forgotten trail; there were still traces of the old trail, for old trails never die they just fade away. As for the women and Raina's boyfriend, they decided to stay there in the car. We walked down the hill to the bottom where the rail tracks lay and on across the old Madrid River; the rocks that cross the river were still crossable, just up the ridge you could see the ruins of the old rock house. As we neared an old tree that still stood there, comes a memory to me, this is where I once stepped on a broken bottle that cut my big toe on the top of my right foot that bled profusely and remembered how hard it was to stop the bleeding. I was about 4 or 5, I still have that scar, my sister Frances was with me that day as she called mother for help. That same tree was where my father and grandfather would hang and slaughter animals for meat. Approaching the rock foundation where the house once stood, there was a wire fence running through the center of the foundation that separated the two private properties that once were my grandparents' ranch house. About 200 feet from the front towards the river were the remains of the old outhouse. At the back of what once was the home of my grandparents was a natural rock formation where I used to play; just to the right from the rocks, about 300 hundred yards is where the goat corral once stood on the hillside. I could go on but, we must leave. As we bid farewell to my grandma's place, we started on our way back to the car. On the way I pointed to a hill across from grandma's place, it was quite a distance to get to the top and remembered that there were many large rocks that surrounded the hilltop, and I also remembered that there was a cave that father had shown me once and saying for me not to go up on my own because of the bats in the cave, including rattlesnakes. We reached the car, and after we ate, we were on our way back to Rania's home. That night after supper, we gathered to discuss the trip. Rania spoke up, telling us that she had taken (stolen) something from the museum and without shame, she took the piece out and showed it to us; as they sat there laughing, I knew that, that antique piece was part of the history of Madrid; this did not sit well with me; now I realize why they separated from the group when we were at the museum where we were told to stay together. Whatever she did with it is unknown. They sat there laughing as I looked over at my wife, she knew my heart was broken, but this was the way they lived, taking, and selling anything they could get their hands on. The only thing one can say is that this was there only way of survival for them when living in poverty. I could say much more but! I will leave it at that. They have all passed on, now it is up to God to do the judging. May they rest in peace.

Chapter 17
Bureau of Indian Affairs

Three days have passed by and still waiting on Adrian to take us to go see my cousins, for I did not know the way. My cousin Wilford cut wind that we were a Raina's place. That afternoon he arrived; it was such welcome site for we had not seen each other since the mid-forties after the WW2 was over. At this time let me tell you about my cousin Wilford! He was a retired US Marine Veteran who fought in the World War Two conflict, a highly decorated Veteran. A well-structured man, and extraordinarily strong but very gentle. We followed Wilford to his home. When we arrived my cousin Blanch and the family were waiting; what a welcome we had. After lunch, Alta and cousin Blanch were getting along knowing each other. Wilford and I went outside as we sat talking about old times, when I noticed an airplane circling around and around over our head; I then asked him if there was an airfield nearby? He said, "No, that is BIA. With curiosity, I asked him who the BIA was. He smiled and said, "That's the Bureau of Indian Affairs, they are keeping a watch on me." I looked at him and laughed; as he replied by saying, "No, no I'm telling you the truth." I looked at him again, he had a very serious look on his face. He then said, "Let me explain." He began by pointing to an open field at the side of the house, it was about five or six acres in length; as I looked, I saw an old tractor with a plowing blade attached to it, and it looked abandoned. He continued saying, "Three years ago we (the family) decided to plow what little land we had left and plant a garden to help us with the food shortage, so we bought that old tractor from an old friend we knew for a couple hundred bucks. A couple of days later, I got up rather early that morning and after breakfast, I climbed on the tractor to warm it up. I had everything ready to go, I put it in gear and started plowing the field; I was about a one quarter way into the field as you can see, I looked up and I saw some men coming towards me. I realized they were ten young Native American Indian men; they walked up to me and demanded for me to get that pile of f-ing shit off their land. Their land! I thought to myself, how could that be? They walk up to me and point at the tractor telling me once again to get that pile of f-ing shit out of their land. They were not playing and demanding for me to get off their land. I knew that the land was given to the family for I had the Land Grant papers given to us by the United States Government many, many years back when the family arrived in the Americas; it was called New Spain Territory, some years later it changed to The New Mexico Territory and was admitted to the union in 1912 when it became the statehood called New Mexico. I jumped off the tractor and no sooner that I landed on the ground that I was jumped and things became serious, I had no choice but to start to defend myself, I dropped a couple of them out cold as the rest jumped in so violently; suddenly one of the fellow got on top of the tractor with a heavy pipe in hand; as he jumped towards me, I saw him coming and I grabbed the pipe and punched him on his way down, he landed on the ground face down; I knew he was hurt badly, the other men stepped back with fear realizing I had the pipe that I had taken away from the guy on the ground. Slowly, one of the fellow bent down to help his friend laying on the ground, he realized that the fellow was not breathing; he looked up at me and screamed out loudly saying, "You, son of a bitch you killed my brother," Things got quiet as they picked the fellow up and walked away cursing at me. I just stood leaning on the tractor with tears in my eyes; I felt awful as to what had just happened. My family walked up to me to comfort me; they did not know that the young man had died in the struggle and not knowing who he was or where they came from. It was midmorning when all this happened; by late afternoon three police cars arrived I was handcuffed and taken away to the Albuquerque city jail. I was accused of aggravated murder. I spent over six weeks in that jail before I went to trial. The trial case lasted for about four weeks; I was pronounced innocent by self-defenses and praying and hoping all this was over; but not so. I was threatened in so many ways that we had to call the authorities, and the only thing they could do was to take me back to Albuquerque for my safety, I was placed in a detention home for my protection. This may sound like a made-up story to you, but the reason is! What I have in my possession, something the local Indian Tribe want; that is the papers I presented at my trial. Now you are probably wondering why that plane is flying around, I have something to show you, see these papers I'm holding in this folder, I must protect them with my life, for these are the legal land grant and the history that has come down through the family form all the many years passed, these are the legal tender titles to the property given to us by the United States Government, and I have to protect them where ever I go; this I was told by the Federal government official. I tried to place them in a safety-deposit box at the bank. The bank called and told me that someone was trying to proclaim my deposit box, right then I decided those papers would be safer in my possession at all times, and I have been carrying them ever since; now, as to why that airplane is flying ever so often is because this is my first three-day vacation from the detention home in over two years in fear that the young Indian tribal men are still after me knowing that I have this papers that I

The Last Padilla Standing

am holding, and to the death of one of their brothers; they seem to have a way of knowing all of my whereabouts. The older local natives wanted all this to come to an end and tried to explain to the younger natives that my grandfather Segura was an Indian agent for the district and he had become blood-brothers with the tribesmen many years back, but this did not fly. When the young tribesmen got the, "I got my rights act" that came about the 1970s, it became a new generation of young native Indians that were claiming that they wanted their land back and this was brought to The Supreme Court; The Supreme Court ruled against us; the bill that went to President Reagan for his signature to return the land to the Pueblo De Cochiti some two miles away, a different tribal group, but you cannot fight city hall." The Cochiti dispute goes back to the days when the southwest was part of the Vice-Royalty (authority of the viceroy) of the New Spain colonies in the new world since 1744; the pueblo, or tribal community had been purchased to what was known as the Santa Cruz Spring Track, a religious area for the tribe, situated southwest of what is now known as Santa Fe, New Mexico. Purchased from the Spaniards who held the title to the land through a Royal Land Grant; nothing to do with where my cousins lived in Sile. All my cousin Wilford wanted to do was to plant a garden on open land where the family has been homesteaded and lived from as far back as the early 1800s. He stood up and said, "Let's go in the house and I'll show you the papers." As we sat around the table, he spread many unusual papers that showed age on sight, and the writing was in incredibly old English and Spanish handwritten. He started to explain each page individually; there were so many Spaniard family names that I could not even pronounce many of them; he went on explaining that; all papers were signed by the government officials of that time. "I wish I could remember some of their names, at least one, but all this happened so suddenly, and I was so overwhelmed. He went on saying every person in the family had their name on file, from the elders' to up-to-date. Cousin Wilford had two brothers, they lived nearby but, they were not involved. He strolled down the list to my name that showed my place of birth and my date of birth, also the rest of the family. This was a unique file and well-written. We spent two nights and one day there. The following day Adrian and my sister arrived ready to leave for home, and that was the last time I spoke to any of my mother's family for they never wrote or called after that. My cousin Blanch made us a great basket of food for us to take along the trip, Adrian took the basket and placed in his car; we bid farewell to all and on our way home. We left early that morning about 7:00 A M. We were well into Arizona, the temperature was 109 and without stopping and we were very hungry, and thirsty. Adrian did not stop for us to eat, he had all the food and water in his car with them. When we were entering Tucson, I got off the freeway and told Alta, "To hell with this, we will stop and eat I will catch up with them, from here I know the way home; we picked up something to eat and drink, it took about forty minutes. As we were on the way. I saw Adrian's car coming back to see why we were not following them. We stopped and waited for him as he made a U-turn; as he came up to my car; he got a little hot under the caller why we were not following him, and I explained to him, that he had all the food and water my cousin Blanch had given us and he would not stop, "we were thirsty, hot, and hungry and you had all the water and food," He did not say much after that, not even an apology, but what the hey it was hot that day, so we went on. It was late and the temperature was getting hotter. We decided to stay overnight in Phoenix, but the weather was about 112 degrees in the rooms, and the rooms did not have air conditioning, only a fan, so we talked it over and decided to go to Baker-Field California. When we arrived there, it was 103 degrees. At 12:00 am. Once again, we talked it over and decided to leave for home. We left about 12:30 that night; I punched my Oldsmobile and made home it in record time as for Adrian, he drove slowly and was left behind. We hit the Bay Area, oh, what a relief it was as we headed home, I felt sorry for my kids and my wife on that miserable ride home. It was well over an hour when my sister called that they were home. We never heard any more about the trip.

Chapter 18
B.A.R.T, the Burial, the Money

I was working for Kawneer on Parr Ave. in North Richmond when I bought my first house on 16th and Market St. in San Pablo Calif. In this house in 1955, this is where my daughter Ellen was born at the Brookside hospital that has been demolished and replaced with the San Pablo Lytton casino. Ellen was about five when we moved to Rose Arbor Ave. my present address. This same hospital is where my other two younger children were born. My son, Timothy in 1964, and my little one Elizabeth born in 1967. I worked at Kawneer for 13 years until Kawneer moved out of town. In 1968. B A R T (Bay Aira Rapped Transit) was just starting, and I placed and application request for work, and without an answer I worked for a few other places after that. I was working for International Harvester; I had been working there for one year or so. One evening I received a phone call from B.A.R.T, to come for an interview at the Richmond shop. It had been over three years since I placed that application with B A R T. I took the following day off to go see what it was all about. I entered the Richmond Shop; a man called Damacio introduced himself as the B A R T's supervisor. His questions were tough, he was looking for specialists not just a mechanic. He went on, then told me that he was looking through my application and saw that I was a glacier that is working with glass. He told me that he was looking for someone to work on the B A R T car windows; that is all it took. The next day, I went to International Harvester and quit. The following week, I started working for B A R T. I was 40 when I started, and this became the best years in my working career. It took me a long while to catch up financially paying off my credit cards and we lived from paycheck to paycheck for a while. Now looking back, pre–B A R T, it was November 6th 1964 when my son Tim was born, and on December 2nd. 1967, Liz came about; my mother-in-law moved in to help Alta; for my daughter Ellen was going to school. A couple of years later Dovie moved to LA to live with her boyfriend Bill. A short time had passed, Atlas's father Herschel was down and out, and he moved in with us for a while again. Now going back further in time! It was 1960 that my father passed away, that left my mother and my grandmother Padilla alone, grandma was blind but mother would not have her put her in a home. I feel bad I never helped my mother like I should have as I did for my wife's parents. Alta was not too close to my mother, maybe it was because Mother's English was not that good so Mother would speak in Spanish with me, and Alta must have felt left out. Mother and Grandma lived in a little shack in 19th St. in San Pablo where they lived alone; my sister lived on 14th St. nearby. Every time I visit Mother it would break my heart. She and grandma did not have much to live on for they lived on welfare and what little Social-Security she received, but never complained. Dovie (my mother-in-law) came back to live with us once again, she was not in good health, after four months or so, she went back to live with Bill in L.A. Dovie passed away on Oct 16th. 1968 in L.A. Bill called us and I took a week off from work to go have her buried there in L A. for we did not have the money to bring and her body here to be buried locally. Bill was a black, ex-military man, he lived in The Watts area there in L. A. The Watts riots were bad back then, and everywhere we went while there, the young black people would look at us until they could see Bill in the car with us. We spent the night at Bill's place. The following day we were to go bury Dovie and meet with Bill at the graveyard, for he was working half day that day. We left his house and I got on the freeway following the city map as to where we were to get off. When I turned on the off-ramp, we ended up heading downtown L A away from the freeway; we were lost and after driving around and around I located the way back to the freeway. By now I knew the car was low on gas again. I found the freeway extent. Just before we got onto the entrance, I saw a gas station and I stopped to gas up. This time I asked the fellow working there if he could tell me how to get to the turn off to the street I was looking for. Again, we were on the way looking for the turn off and as I turned! Uh oh, it looked familiar I was on my way back downtown LA; this time it took me a bit longer looking for the freeway; it took well over a half hour to find the way into the freeway entrances again, I looked at my gas gauge and I was almost at half tank, my Oldsmobile was a gas guzzler, once again I was back at the same gas station and the same gas attended; after the tank was full, I felt like a fool asking him once more, he looked up at me and smiled and said, "You are not from around here are you?" I told him where we were from and about Dovie, this time he told me that the off-ramp had a three-street turn off on it, and that I had taken the first one that went downtown and that the ramp had two more turn off up a head and for me to be sure I took the third one. We finally got there; and not too far off was the cemetery where Bill was waiting for us. We had to pay for a casket; I told the care tender that we had to go with a popper casket, he held back then he spoke up and told me that he had a cancelation on a very nice white casket, and he would let us have it for the same price of a popper casket, the cost was at $500. I had to buy it on my credit card; so, done. After the business was over, we were talking with Bill, when he told us that Dovie had a little money in the bank and that Alta was the only one who could take the money out. Strange that he took this long to mention about the money, and that Alta was the only one that could take the money out. That left me wondering that he must have tried to retrieve the money and the bank knew something was not right. We followed Bill back to his home; he got in the car with us, and on to the bank in the Watts area where the bank was so Alta could retrieve the cash of some $3100.00. It was not a safe area to be around due to the Watts riots, but we were with Bill. When we arrived at the bank, Alta and Bill went in, it so happened the bank teller told Alta that she was not of age and that she could not take the money out; this was strange, I believe it was because Bill was with her, and they knew that he tried to retrieve the money a few days back. She was told that her father was the only one able to redeem the cash. We followed Bill back to his home, and we readied our stuff and said goodbye to Bill and headed home. The following weekend, we took my father-in-law Hatchel; this time we did not have Bill with us. We made it to the bank, I parked as close as I could to the bank door, where I could see them. My father-in-law was a smart-ass white boy and acting stupid in the bank, and embarrassing Alta. They retrieved the money and got into the car, I started to go, and as we were nearing the street exit a couple of cars full of black guys tried to block us off, reasons unknown, other that my father-in-law acting foolish in the bank. I remembered my racing techniques in a tight spot, I punched the gas paddle on my Oldsmobile and over the embankment I managed to out drive them and on to the freeway. My two kids, Tim, Liz, and my wife were very frightened. As for my father-in-law? Not a word out of his smart mouth was spoken that almost got us in a huge mess in the middle of the LA Watt riots. As for me, I had a cool head and made it back to the free-way and home bound. When we got home a week or so later, Alta starts getting mail from Bill, threatening her for the money, unknown how he found out that Alta had gotten the money, we never found out; he would write letters to my wife and this she kept to herself for she did not want me to know that she was sending Bill money; I was wondering where all her money was going for, she had not bought anything of value other than paying the $500.00' to the bank for her mother's funeral. I talked it over with her, she finally told me that Bill had threatened her over the money; we talked it over and this brought a little fear to us for we knew Bill was unpredictable, we talked it over and I decided to buy a weapon, so I bought a 38-special pistol with fear of Bill's temperament. Back then, one did not have to wait for a permit for a weapon, it was pay and take. What we did not know is that her aunt Boots was in cahoots with Bill over the jealousy of the money Alta had received. The following Saturday we went to visit her aunt Boots and they were not at home. As we were ready to leave a close friend of Boots who lived next door saw us and told us that Boots and Arval had gone to LA and meet with Bill for weekend; this was rather strange for Boots did not mentioned anything to Alta about going to see Bill; and to this day what they talked about with Bill is unknown. Boots never told Alta that they had gone to LA to meet with Bill. Later that week, Alta received a letter from Bill how he had taken care of Dovie and deserve the cash. Alta gave most of the money to Bill, after that, she did not hear from him ever again; as for her aunt Boots, she never mentation anything about the trip to LA, mum's the word. The only thing we got from that money were four tires for my car about $200.00 and a 38 special for $69.00 and the $500.00 cash to pay the bill at the bank for my mother-in-law 'casket, and well over $2000.00 went to Bill. I got a little hot under the collar, but I realized Alta was right. I felt sorry for my wife for she took a lot of crap from her side of her family, but we kept this to ourself. Alta and all her family are all deceased, and I still hold a negative feeling with all the crap her family had given her, may God forgive them, and forgive me for the negative thoughts that ran through my mind periodically.

Chapter 19
Final Chapter: Life Goes On

Now! What about a little happiness into the story. We moved to our recent home, here on Rose Arbor. In September first of 1961. Ellen started school the following semester at the River Side School down the hill from where we lived; she and her girl friend named Harlen McDaniel would take the school bus to school every morning. Within the year Ellen had made many friends here on the hill other than Harlen, there were, Pamela, (Pam) Eline, and three sisters, Patricia, Nice, and Beebe, and a few more. Time passed on; one evening the girls were in their preteen years and having an overnight party here at our home; they were having a great time playing spook night. Patricia was having a make-believe seance, saying, "Oh, spirits talk to me," They were having a great time; I was sitting in the kitchen reading the newspaper and listening to them, when an idea popped into my mind, I was going to have fun with the girls, they were all sitting in a circle; in front of the couch; Patricia was sitting facing them and going on with the seance saying, "Oh spirits talk to me," as she carried on speaking to the spirits; I sneaked behind the couch as I responded by saying, "What do you want." God bless them (and shame on me,) they all jumped screaming scared that the ghostly spirit had answered Patricia. I feel so guilty and ashamed, for my niece Debby really got very frightened that night. After much laughter, things settled down. Ellen still talks about that night and another event that comes to mind with the girls. One evening the girls were downstairs it was Ellen's 16th birthday, they were having a great time; Tim was about seven, when he came and asked me for my small flashlight, he said he was making something for the girls downstairs; he had a plastic pumpkin head left from the past Halloween, he shaped it like a ghostly body and placed a cape made from an old thin curtain Alta was throwing away; the flashlight went in the pumpkin's head, and he placed a blond wig that Ellen use to play with; it took him while to make. When finished, he invited me to go upstairs to his room with him; not knowing what he had in mind, I followed him. He stood there holding the pumpkin and asked me to open the window and remove the screen, suddenly! I realized what he had in mind. I just shook my head in amazement; from his bedroom window he slowly lowered the pumpkin and started to sway it side to side, the wind was waving the cape slowly. When one of the girls spotted the ghost and started screaming; as they crowded the stairway to the upper room, when Tim came down from his room laughing; the girls were somewhat angry but soon it became a peal of laughter and back to somewhat normal. School had started, Tim was almost eight years of age; one night we went to a parent's school meeting at the Riverside School, as the meeting went on some Cub Scout Dignitaries were there looking for volunteers to start a Cub Scout group at Riverside School. No one in the room raised their hand. Tim looked up at me saying, "Dad why don't you raise your hand?" I looked at him and shook my head and said no. Tim looked back up at me with a sad look on his face, as I just looked at him and slowly raised my hand not releasing what I had just volunteered for and not knowing anything about Cub Scouting! What a welcome came about in that room as I became the Cubmaster of a new Cub Scout troop in 1972. I was working graveyard with Friday and Saturday off and that went well with our weekend meetings. One of the men, whose son was in my pack, was named Jim Ogawa, became the spoke man for our pack; I named our pact, "Pact 777"; and was accepted by the Boy Scouts Association of America. We became well known by the Boy Scouts Association for we won many events, more than any other pact around. I have a scrapbook with many memories of the gatherings, and golden dinners I had with my son, my little girl Liz, and my wife Alta, who became Den Mother for troop number two and my little girl, Liz, became the Princess of Pack 777. The scrapbook I made, was for my son Timothy that was so cherished, by him. (He passed on 01/30/2019) now, I have it back in my possession, that brings a tear in my eyes when I look at it. Our pact 777 participated in May events where we placed first place many times. Mr. Jim Ogawa was now the representative for my Pack. After more than three years of cub scouting, Tim picked a new tarn, bike-motocross on bicycles he was very good at it and many Bike-motocross clubs wanted Tim to join. But he had more fun beating them on his own. After a time, at thirteen he picked up the guitar he was doing so well that I bought him a very well-built Japanese copy of a Fender that I replaced the two pickups and parts with original Fender parts that one could not tell the difference except for the fretboard that had a fret at the very top of the fretboard not found in American made guitars. The guitar turns out very well. As time went on, he traded the guitar for a white Gibson he so cherished that I now have as a keepsake along with his Marshall amp.; memories that dwell deep in my heart). As life went on, we lived on the hillside overlooking the bay; my youngest daughter Liz (Elizbeth) was about four years of age; one day, I had to go get some parts from the hardware store that used to be about three blocks from San Pablo Avenue and the Dam Road near a bar called The Lighthouse inn, that use to be a landmark from back in time, I needed to fix the kitchen sink, I had the water turned off; anyway Liz wanted to go with me and I told her no, for I was in a hurry knowing that if she went with me she would want to look at the toys and I was in a hurry to get the water back on; so, I went on and left her crying, I felt bad but time was not on my side. As I Was picking up the parts that I had a hard time finding some of them. When I felt someone pulling my pant leg I looked down, and next to me was Liz, she had a big smile on her face; she had walked down the hill, down the Dam Road to where the hardware store was near San Pablo Ave. This scared me some, but I could not get mad at her for she showed me the love she had for me, she was my side buddy. When we got home, I had a little talk with her, and I told her about the danger that she could have been in. She got up and placed he arms around my leg and told me that she was sorry. There are so many memories I have stored in my mind but! This book would be as thick as an encyclopedia dictionary. We never had much money just a credit card that was at the max most of the time. When vacation came, I did not have the money to take my kids to places like Disneyland, so every time vacation came about, we would go camping; we always had a good time, but I still feel sad not being able to have taken them to other places. The only time we went to Disneyland was when Tim was four, Liz was going on two, Ellen was in her teens; as we entered the park, we were looking at a marching band nearby when, suddenly an opening came out off the ground. Oh yes, Mickey Mouse came out of a manhole nearby where we were standing. Tim had on his Buster Brown Tee shirt and shorts he looked so cute as he stood there, looking so great, Tim looked up and saw Mickey, he grabbed ahold of my leg with much fear for the only Mickey Mouse he ever knew off was the little one he had at home. The one here at Disney was well over six feet tall. Mickey pointed with his finger motioning for Tim to come to him; Tim just held on tighter to my leg. The Page girl came up to me and told me that Mickey was to pick a child to go on the parade with him and he picked Tim of all the kids around, Mickey tried so hard to convince Tim to come over to him, but Tim was so frightful hanging on to my leg. After a while, Mickey placed his hands on his waist and shrugged his shoulders and walked away like he was sad, suddenly as he turned and looked back at Tim and pretended to wipe the tears from his eyes. The crowd cheered and Tim held on tighter. Mickey had to pick another child. As for my Liz? She took Ice skating lessons, Ballet, and girl scouting; I could go on with many stories of my family, but you would not be able to hold this book in one hand. As for my daughter Ellen, she was already a young lady into the life of womanhood, she was into ballet, and performing on stage. Along that time, I taught her how to drive. Life goes on here at Rose Arbor Ave. As I sit here with the beautiful memories for over sixty years plus, here is where my home stands. My walls are full of pictures with many many tears from the past, as I sit here writing my memoirs and thankful to God as I go on. Now comes the time for you to think of when you and your spouse were young never knowing what the future will be like when you reach 89 years of age as I am. Talk with your kids, let them know what time was like when you were young let them know the history of your family, because Father time is creeping up on you, tell them about the good times and the sad times; these are the times that go deep into their minds in wonderment. I am grateful with what God has given me. I am an artist, a musician, and a writer, although my age has cut up with me, I am still actively writing, and with my artworks, and I play my steel guitar here at home every so often. As for my daughters, they keep in touch with me by phone. I retired from B A R T in 1997. I would have worked a few more years but my wife Alta was extremely ill, and I became her caregiver 24/7, for I could not place her in a medical care home, she passed on August 12, 2005. It had been 14 years passed her death, when, another tragic moment happened in my life, my only son Timothy passed away suddenly on January 30 2019 he was 55 years of age; he died on the job working for B A R T. He lived with me, he told me that he did not want me to live alone, but God had another plan for him; now all I have are great memories of my wife and my son Timothy. Now I am left with my two girls, Ellen Meza and Lizabeth White, and one great-grandson named Andrew White and two great sons-in-law, Cavin, and Ralph this is all I have left in my life. Andrew and I have great memories of when he was a little fellow, and I used to babysit him. I bought him a few Lionel trains and we spent many hours on the floor laying out a train station and a long track in the hallway. He is now twenty-one and a college graduate, he is so intelligent he reminds me of my father with how well-educated they both have been, as for Andrew he is well on his way to manhood. Now I am sitting here with tears of time passed and with all the many memories of yesteryear. No, I am not ready to give up I will see a great grandson or a great, granddaughter one day. It is time for me to stop writing my memoirs. All this I have written are with memories of my son Timothy Andrew who asked me if I would write a biography of the family's past; sad to say, he never had a chance to read what I have written about my past. Now, I pass my memories on to my two girls, Ellen, and Elizabeth in memories of their beloved brother Timothy Andrew Padilla. May he rest in peace.

What I have written in this novel, is to the best of my memories of my yesteryears. Amazing how well I can remember all this in detail as if it were only yesterday. All that I have written in this novel is with honesty and gratefulness that God has given me. If I have insulted anyone in the family, forgive me. So ends my journey in my God-given life.

Photo Album

This was the realistic manger with real animals

The three Kings on the way to Bethlehem on the hill are site just below the Bethlehem display on the hill site

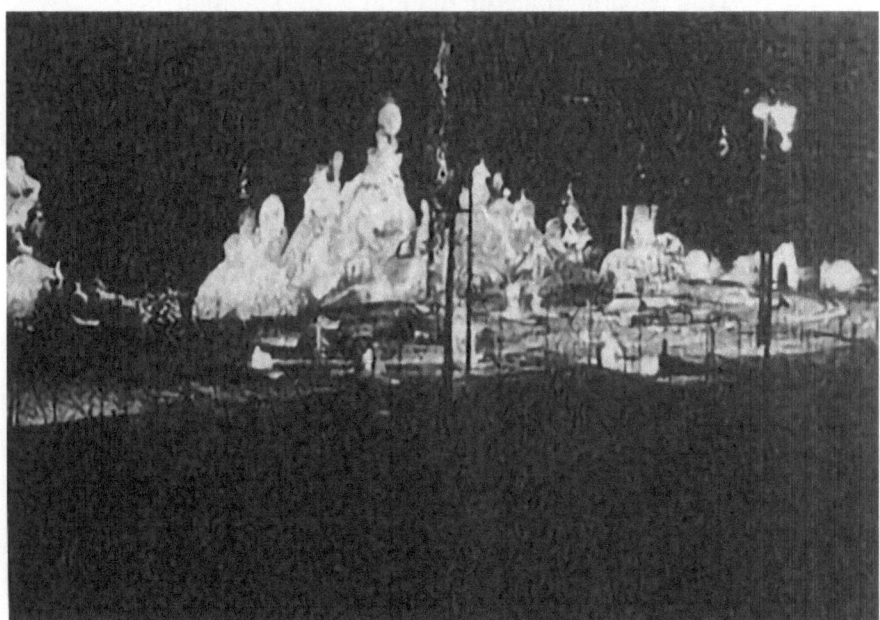

These were the famous Christmas decorated scenes at the ballpark every Christmas, all ended December 7, 1941 due to the World War II action

These are the two crosses given to me and my sister Frances by mother

Chrismas view of Front Street and the town's display at night

The welcome entrance on the south side of Madrid

The display of the Choir Boys on the hill site

Company store at Christmas time

Meat Market

View of Madrid from the North

View from the South side

Madrid Miners Baseball Team in 1930s

Madrid ball Park

"The Last Padilla Standing."

This novel was written for my son
TIMOTHY ANDREW PADILLA.

Rest in peace

END

www.ingramcontent.com/pod-product-compliance
Lightning Source LLC
LaVergne TN
LVHW040152080526
838202LV00042B/3129